SPARE-TIME STEPS
TO YOUR FIRST MILLION

Spare-Time Steps
To Your First Million

Bill Hammond

Parker Publishing Company, Inc.

West Nyack, New York

© 1979, *by*

PARKER PUBLISHING COMPANY, INC.

West Nyack, N.Y.

Library of Congress Cataloging in Publication Data

Hammond, Bill.
    Spare-time steps to your first million.

    Includes index.
    1. Success. 2. Business. 3. Selling. 4. Self-
employed. I. Title.
HF5386.H244   650'.12   78-10359
ISBN 0-13-824219-4

Printed in the United States of America

WHAT THIS BOOK WILL DO FOR YOU

You are about to take the first steps to incredible wealth. Simple steps that will bring you thousands and thousands of dollars. Steps taken by such people as Fletcher J. who started with an investment of $100, and in ten years built his spare-time interest into an international electronics company worth more than $53 million. People such as Joe L. took such steps, and his ideas have so far brought him more than $500,000. Reg M.'s income has already reached $85,000 a year and is increasing at a colossal rate.

This book is for people who want to make a lot of money, immense sums of money, enough money to make every dream they've ever had come true. Take a moment to think of some of the things you would do or buy if you had unlimited wealth. You'd be able to buy that beautiful dream house you've often talked about, or perhaps a new car or a vacation home in the mountains or at the beach. You would be able to indulge your hobbies and pleasures; music, art, travel. In fact, you would be able to do just about anything you wanted to do. The world would be your playground.

Most spare-time occupations are easy to get into. It's the way you conduct the venture that makes all the difference. Can you imagine starting a spare-time business repairing bicycles in your garage? Seems easy enough doesn't it? And that's exact-

ly how Herby R. started. Within a few years he had a 40' luxury
cruiser, a Rolls Royce Silver Cloud, and was able to take an extended trip around the world and still come back to a six figure
bank balance. Benito F., a penniless immigrant from Puerto
Rico, climbed out of the ghetto to build himself a $4 million
corporation that operates in three states. How? He makes
fences.

What did these men have in common? They had a strong
desire to become wealthy. They both wanted the security and
comfort of a very large bank balance, and they both discovered
the secret of success. A prosperous and flourishing business is
well within your reach, and starting it in your spare time is a
safe and logical way to lay the foundation.

But don't ever be misled. Spare-time big business is not the
exclusive domain of any particular group of people. Anyone can
do it, regardless of race, sex or religion; anyone can build a
spare-time business with an income that would give many
corporation executives an inferiority complex. Even age has
little to do with spare-time success.

Louis M. started an import business at the age of seventy.
He began by borrowing a small amount of money from his son.
The son didn't really expect the loan to be repaid, but thought it
would give the older man "something to do." By the time Louis
died at the age of 85, his bank balance stood at more than two
million dollars.

Education also seems to have little bearing on success.
Although a few of today's millionaires inherited their money,
most self-made millonaires, and incidentally, more than a few
were high school dropouts, pushed their way into the six figure
income bracket by selecting a venture which interested them,
and then finding an "angle" which took them into the millionaire class.

You will discover that making big money is exciting.
Operating a successful, high-profit enterprise provides an
exhileration which is endless and utterly satisfying. No matter

what your background or interests, somewhere in this book you will find an idea, a scheme, which will hit you with the power of a striking baracuda. You will be fired with an irresistible urge to get started, and at that point, SPARE-TIME STEPS TO YOUR FIRST MILLION will guide you step-by-step along well-tested paths. When you are ready it will aim you at the target with the accuracy of a laser beam. Nothing will be able to stand in your way.

There's an old saying, and it's the second of the success secrets, that "Money makes money," and as you read this book you will quickly realize the truth of that adage.

The money you make will pyramid into great wealth with hardly any effort on your part. Once the big money snowball starts rolling, you will become little more than a spectator, watching it grow and grow in size.

If you truly want that million dollars, or even just a portion of it, the first move has to come from you. No one will ever make it for you.

Make that move today. This book will show you how. I promise.

Bill Hammond

Table of Contents

Contents

Chapter 1

How To Unleash That Dynamic Potential— Spare Time

You have the ability to make more money than you will ever need. You have the potential of turning your most impossible daydreams into reality and assuring yourself of an income which will keep you in comfort for the rest of your life. Need proof? Read on.

Bob M. works as a department manager in a large store, a job he has held for 14 years. A little over three years ago he had the opportunity to buy the remainder of a line of toys that had been priced to sell in the store at $15.95. In order to move them out to make room on the shelves for fresh merchandise that would sell faster, they sold all 27 boxes of toys to Bob as a job lot for $100.

The following Sunday morning, Bob took them to a local open air market and displayed them, together with a large sign that said, "Manufacturer's close out. Reg. $15.95; while they last, $8." Within two hours all 27 had been sold. The next day, Bob telephoned the manufacturer and asked if they had any more of those toys or any other lines they would care to sell him on a cash basis. They said they would be prepared to offer three other lines and suggested a price that Bob thought was more than reasonable.

Gradually, as his market selling developed, Bob M. approached other manufacturers, taking on a wide variety of different merchandise all priced to sell well below the original store price. Within a few months, Bob's wife was running a second stall in another market and selling on Tuesdays and Thursdays. Today, Bob has 22 stalls in nearby towns and has people selling for him every day of the week. He continues to hold down his job in the department store, but he spends his spare time organizing a business which has provided him every week with an income that is three times his monthly store salary.

The phrase "Time is money" is an old cliché but it has never been more true than in this modern day struggle to succeed. Every spare minute can literally be turned into hard cash, and if you are interested in such luxuries as an extended tour of the world, your own jet plane, a gracious home with tennis courts and swimming pool, or even the simple satisfaction of having enough money to be able to retire without fear of financial difficulties—the time and great wealth go hand in hand, and you're on your way to your first million.

THE FIRST STEP TOWARD A SECURE FUTURE

Eileen R. earns $125 a week as a typist in her regular employment. In six months, though, she has built a spare-time business for herself that brings her an extra $400 a week and is growing at a fantastic rate every day.

A plastics company employs **Rex B.** as a traveling salesman. In his spare time he is president of a rapidly expanding import business. Ten years ago, Don R. worked as a lathe operator in a large factory. Today he owns two factories twice the size. What is the single success factor shared by these and so many other people that you'll be meeting as you progress through the book? What secret knowledge enables them to build and develop a business with a multi-million dollar potential?

They discovered a simple formula. They learned how to turn their spare time into hard cash. They discovered how to take that first spare-time step to a fortune. You too can take that step, but to do so you have to fulfill one rigid and exacting condition—one uncompromising stipulation—if you want all the pleasures that a great deal of money can bring.

You must want to take that first step. You must be positively certain that you want to launch yourself into a new and exciting lifestyle. Think about it first, then if you're sure that's what you really want to do, let's get started.

Settle down in a comfortable armchair with a note pad and pencil. Make it a time and place when you'll not be disturbed for an hour or so and be prepared to do a little self-appraisal.

Lean back and relax for a minute or two until your mind settles down. Get used to the feeling, you'll be doing quite a bit of it in the future. This state of mind is the basis for all the money which will soon be accumulating in your bank account—relaxing and thinking.

Now it's time to start making a few notes. First, write down two dates. One six months from now and the other twelve months from now. Alongside the first date write in an amount which is double the wages that you'll have brought home during that six months in your regular job. Alongside the second date write a figure four times that of your yearly take-home pay.

These are your target figures. They're trifling amounts and you're going to pass them without too much trouble. In fact, three years from now you'll wonder why you aimed so low. If you were to aim at the figure which is really within your capability it would be so high you'd have difficulty believing it.

Next, write down the amount of time that you'll be able to put aside each week. Be as accurate as you can because your future calculations are going to be based on this estimation. Take into account that weekly ball game you can't miss and the weekends you visit relatives or they visit you. You may find it easier to arrive at a more accurate estimation if you break it down into hours per day and days per week.

The third figure you need, and it's probably going to be difficult to assess, is how much cash per week you'll be able to invest in your project until it starts returning a profit. Don't be too concerned if it's only a couple of dollars, some of today's well-known businesses literally started from scratch.

It's not so much a matter of having a great deal of money, it's more a case of knowing how to make the most of what you do have. One of your greatest assets isn't money at all, it's the knowledge that you carry around in your head.

THE 15 MINUTE QUIZ THAT COULD CHANGE YOUR LIFE

We have reached the most important part of your self-appraisal—the part wherein your treasure trove is buried.

Make two lists—one, a list of your skills, knowledge and abilities, and the other of your hobbies and interests.

The first list will include various jobs you have held, the positions you reached and skills which you may now take for granted. List the fact that you can drive a school bus, that you were a pilot during the war, or that you lived in a foreign country for some time—any specialized knowledge that you have gained.

The second list will contain hobbies and interests; past, present and projected. List every pastime in which you have ever become involved; some you may even have forgotten until you start thinking back. These skills and interests can play a vital part in your future.

Eileen W. owed her success to a fleeting stint as an in-store cookery demonstrator. She chanced to read in her local paper about TVP—meat-like fibers made from soybean.

The article stated that the food product was almost entirely protein and would be a valuable addition to the family meals. One pound of TVP could be added to three pounds of hamburger meat as an extender, not only improving the food value but also considerably reducing the cost of the meal.

She made a few enquiries and managed to obtain a small quantity of TVP as a sample. She was so impressed that she went back to the processing plant and told them that she wanted to buy wholesale and act as a distributor. The product was new and there was still the question of how the public would receive it, so they told her that she could have as much as she wanted at 30¢ a pound in 50 lb. sacks.

Eileen thought she knew a winner when she saw it. She arranged for credit to be established and bought ten sacks. Within a week it had all been sold to friends and neighbors at 45¢ a pound and orders were coming in for more. She went back to the supplier, paid her bill and asked them to deliver 50 more sacks of TVP; but these quantities she wanted at 25¢ a pound. They agreed.

Over the next few months she expanded her spare-time business to include other dehydrated foods processed by the same firm. At the same time, she began stocking plastic food containers (for which she paid 50¢ and sold at 90¢), books on cookery and various flavoring extracts.

At first she worked from her home, but it became necessary to rent a small store. She found one in a shopping center which she could rent for $75 a month. She began by opening for two hours every evening and all day Saturday and Sunday.

Between 2:00 P.M. and 3:00 P.M. every Saturday she would hold cookery demonstrations, showing her customers how to get the best from the products she offered. On an average weekend, she now anticipates selling at least $700 worth of food products, giving her a weekly gross of more than $1,000. Her profit has grown steadily since the day she started.

Rex B. started his spare-time business almost by accident. He owes it to the knowledge acquired in a previous job when he worked as a buyer for a small chain store.

His spare-time venture started when Steve C., one of the customers on whom he was calling, mentioned that his feet were aching. It appeared that Steve suffered from a slight deformity of the toes and buying comfortable shoes was a problem. He had even gone to the expense of having shoes handmade, but was still unable to get the comfort he needed.

Rex remembered receiving a catalogue from Japan and one of the items they had offered was handmade shoes. As a courtesy to Steve, he suggested that if he were given a sketch of the outline of Steve's foot together with the measurements, he might be able to get a pair of shoes made for him.

When the shoes arrived they proved to be so satisfactory that Steve ordered two more pairs, but this time insisted on paying. The price was about a third of what he had previously paid.

This encouraged Rex to enquire about other items he could buy from Japan. Within two years, working with his two sons and son-in-law, Rex B. has established a thriving import business, specializing in handmade clothing and selling almost entirely by mail order. Every week he mails out 2,000 beautifully illustrated brochures provided by his Japanese suppliers.

Rex B.'s income has leapt from $1,200 a month to $10,000 and he says that he's only just beginning to scratch the surface.

Everybody has knowledge which they have accumulated from day to day experience. This knowledge, when directed into the right channels, is as valuable as a six-figure checking account. The hobbies and recreations in which you are interested have provided you with an enormous amount of knowledge.

Next time you get into a conversation with a fellow enthusiast, stand back and listen to yourself talk. Your fund of knowledge on those things which interest you is immense. You have anecdotes ready to relate about other people with similar interests, you know every store in town that caters to your special hobbies, and without doubt you have several books and magazines on the shelves in your home or office which are a source of new ideas. Your hobby is part of your life and it can provide a means of filling that life with luxury.

HOW YOUR HOBBY CAN TRIPLE YOUR INCOME

Study your list of hobbies and recreational interests and ask yourself what products, service or instruction would improve any of those hobbies. For the moment, don't worry about the problems of bringing about those improvements; just concentrate on ways to make your hobby or recreation more pleasurable.

Typical examples which have recently appeared on the market are: the thermometer which will read the temperature at any pre-determined depth of water, providing invaluable information for the serious angler; chessmen with the moves made by each piece molded on to the base, to help novice players; and equalizers which enable the music enthusiast to match is hi-fi components to suit room acoustics. It will make speakers sound better and help eliminate hiss and scratch from all recordings.

The market for products connected with hobbies and recreational activities is immense, and is one of the easiest in which to get started.

Joy H. is 25 years old. Three years ago she won a trip to Italy for herself and her husband, Fred. It would have been a long time before his job as a bookkeeper or hers as a clerk in a department store could have provided them with an opportunity for such a vacation; but what Joy and Fred H. saw on the beaches of the Italian Riviera projected them into a spare-time business that was to change their entire way of living.

The bikinis and men's swimwear they saw was so striking and exciting that Joy and Fred first decided to try and import them for sale in America. However, during the two weeks they were there, their ideas crystallized into a slightly different form.

Why try to import the swimwear and be satisfied with a retailer's profit? Joy felt sure they could manufacture similar models themselves. She and Fred spent the remainder of their vacation taking as many photographs on the beaches that they could, and as soon as they returned home Joy tried to copy the styles and patterns that had proved so interesting.

The swimwear turned out as well as she and Fred had hoped, but merchandising them was a failure. The few stores which would agree to stock them, sold the new designs steadily; but the larger stores were reluctant to handle them.

One day, after some more of their samples had been returned with a disheartening "No thank you," Joy said, "I think we ought to forget it for awhile. Perhaps we've been pushing too hard."

They tried to put the problem aside, and then one morning Joy awoke with the answer clear in her mind. It was so obvious that they wondered why they hadn't seen it long before.

Today, four years later, their small factory makes nothing but swimwear to their special design. It is then packed by a firm of packaging specialists and sent on to a warehouse ready for shipping to a marketing area where they have established a firm foothold. They send their swimwear to Italy.

Since Joy and Fred H. made their first visit, she has been back to Italy three times to open further outlets for their American-made "Italian" swimwear, and there are signs that they are now beginning to break into some of the American markets.

Although Joy has since left her job as a sales clerk in order to start a family, Fred still works as a bookkeeper and helps Joy manage the swimwear business in his spare time.

Don R.'s approach to spare-time money was entirely different. He is one of those people whose work is also his hobby.

He worked as a lathe operator in a factory during the day and had his own modest engineering shop in the basement of his house. It was here that he spent most of his spare time.

Helping a woman change a wheel on a camper gave Don his first idea. He saw how difficult it was to get the spare wheel out from under the body of the truck, and the even greater difficulty of storing away the old wheel.

Don went back to his home workshop and devised a gear and cable arrangement which made the whole operation so simple that it became practically effortless.

He advertised his invention in recreational magazines and then subcontracted the orders he received to his employer. The parts, which he assembled himself, cost $4, and he sold the completed article at $24.95.

The recreational field proved a profitable market for Don and he concentrated on devising gadgets which would make for carefree camping—items such as collapsible steps, mud deflectors and hydraulic jacks.

His ideas caught on and in three years Don R. had made enough money to start his own factory. Now his profits were much higher. He no longer had to subcontract his orders and as his business grew he expanded his advertising program and spent more time on promoting further gadgets. Today he has two factories—one engineering and one plastics. The results of his spare-time activity may be seen in practically every campground across the nation.

By now you will have probably noted a few ideas of your own against the two lists you have compiled. Shortly, you will learn how to convert those ideas into dollar bills. For the moment, let's consider marketing. Every new idea, new product and new service needs marketing.

MERCHANDISING WITH A DIFFERENCE

Telephone selling has been one of the most effective methods of merchandising almost since the time telephones became part of the American lifestyle. It reaches the potential customer in his home and it enables the salesman to use his personality—an important factor not possible with direct mail selling or mail order.

Mary H. discovered almost by accident that she had a telephone sales personality. She worked as a secretary for a small plastics factory that made artificial flowers and fruit. For a while business was good and the factory buzzed with activity. Gradually, however, business began to decline and the owner of the factory looked around for a way of stimulating sales. He decided that instead of selling his flowers and fruit as separate varieties, he would mold a series of plastic baskets and containers and sell his product carefully arranged into table centerpieces.

This plan seemed doomed to failure. The merchants who had previously handled his merchandise were now turning to different lines which they hoped would boost their own sagging sales. Although they agreed the floral arragements were attractive, they were not willing to re-stock that type of product.

As business continued to falter, Mary H. could see her job being jeopardized. She became even more concerned because she thought that the new product was so attractive that if only the housewives could see it, they would buy it. Almost in desperation she telephoned a few of her friends and told them of the new items being manufactured by the company for which she worked. The friends were interested and asked if they could see some of the samples. Within a few weeks, Mary had sold more than 50 floral arrangements and her employer agreed to supply them to her at wholesale prices. As her experience grew, Mary H. expanded her area of operations and found that she could sell to complete strangers merely by giving a verbal description of how the new table floral basket could add to the room decor.

Mary's next step was to advertise in out-of-town newspapers, offering a new line for people who would like to sell by telephone. Today she has 32 people in various parts of the country selling the floral arrangements. She gets five percent commission on every item sold by her sales people and already her monthly income is in the four figure bracket.

If you would like to try telephone selling, almost any manufacturer of domestic products will make their merchandise available to you. First decide on the type of products you think you could sell, enquire of one or two of the manufacturers about the lines in which you are interested, and tell them that you would like to try selling their product by means of telephone sales.

A few manufacturers may object, but there are many who will see in your offer an opportunity to increase their own outlets. The profit you make will be determined by the price at which you can buy and the price at which you sell. You will soon discover that telephone selling has its own special techniques—it's always interesting and can be amazingly profitable.

One of the techniques you will be using is put in the form of questions that are the basis of every sale ever made.

THE THREE W'S OF BIG MONEY

Every successful business, including such giants as Ford, Singer, Sony and General Electric, is based on an answer to the three W's or Who Wants What?

You can spend thousands of dollars developing the most ingenious equipment to enable people to stand on their heads, but if no one wants to buy it, you'll never sell it. It's such an obvious statement that you'll probably be saying to yourself, "Well everyone knows that," but every year hundreds of people try to start a business with products, which to say the least, are difficult to sell.

If you are going to take those first vital steps that lead to the very big money, you need to know who wants to buy, what they want to buy and where you can obtain it. The answer to the first question can be answered very quickly. Everyone wants to buy. We are always buying something. The answer to the second question is the big money answer, but it is one which is not too difficult to provide.

The items which people want to buy are offered month after month by the hundreds of magazines so neatly displayed in the supermarkets, drugstores and libraries. Each magazine is carefully slanted to a specific section of the public and each section has its own buying requirements. If you want to know who buys what, the answer is accurately provided by magazines.

From this point you can work backwards or forwards. You can either devise or search for a product which will fall into any section which interests you or, alternatively, you may have already stumbled across an interesting item which you think will sell, but need to know to whom you can offer it.

The magazines will provide you with all the information you need to start your selling campaign. A study of the advertising in magazines which are devoted to a specific section of the public will tell you not only which items are currently popular, but how they are being offered. It is information which marketing services will provide for a considerable fee, but it is knowledge which you can obtain for yourself with a little time and perseverance. With this information available to you, it is not too difficult to select a product which will sell to the type of market that has a special interest for you.

For example, Eric D. is a keen fresh water fisherman, and when one of his fiberglass fishing rods was cracked by accident, he decided that since the manufacturer was fairly close by he would take it back personally and ask if they could repair it quickly. During conversation he discovered that the firm was also venturing into a new product,—fiberglass golf clubs with an extremely practical design.

To Eric D., those golf clubs represented an entirely new future. Although at that time the clubs were in the experimental stage, Eric asked if he could have exclusive sales and distribution rights. The firm had already established outlets for its fishing tackle, but it had not yet decided how they were going to handle the distribution of the golf clubs.

Eric D. impressed them with his tremendous enthusiasm and they agreed that he could sell them on an exclusive, but provisional basis. It was all that Eric needed. His advertisements, small at first, began to appear in newspapers and magazines and he began making personal weekend calls on as many golf clubs as he could contact. Today, Eric D.'s income runs into the thousands and he has 12 different products on the market, all printed with his special trademark.

HOW TO BUILD A GOOD IDEA INTO A FORTUNE

You've had your idea, you know your market and you think you know its potential. Now you want to know how to get started turning that idea into a fortune. Dave G. can show you one way.

In England at the end of World War II, fiberglass products began to make their appearance. Dave had very little money, but he had a good idea. He visited a manufacturer of store window manikins who had just converted from paper mache models to fiberglass. Dave asked if he could have a few sample products made. He told them that he wanted the products shaped like a German soldier's helmet, and drew a sketch of what he wanted. He also explained that he couldn't pay for the models, but perhaps the manufacturer would be interested in a proposition.

He offered the manufacturer ten percent of the profit on all sales plus the exclusive rights to manufacture this part of the product. His proposition was accepted and the cost of the product was established at approximately $1 each.

He then visited a manufacturer of leather goods, explained what he wanted and made a similar offer which was also accepted. Again, his cost was established at approximately $1.

The result was a motorcycle crash helmet styled as one had never been styled before. It was the beginning of the "space age look" for motorcyclists.

At $10 each, the helmets became popular overnight. The demand far outstripped anything that Dave had ever imagined. After a while, competitive models made their appearance, but Dave G. was perfectly content. He was firmly established and already into his next idea. Today he owns a large house in an exclusive part of London and has ten new projects earning him money at the moment.

Selling is now much easier than it was a few years ago. Potential customers are constantly exposed to new ideas and progressive designs. They expect continual improvement in every aspect of modern living and they are prepared to pay for those improvements.

THE READY-MADE MARKETS

Because your potential customers have been so exposed to clever and persuasive advertising, they have become very receptive to the idea of trying new products. Therefore, any new service or device you would like to offer will not have to be launched on a completely cold market. Although you may find it difficult to believe at this time, there are people actually waiting and wanting to try your product.

The main route to these interested people is once again through magazines. This time you are concentrating on those markets which are already well established, the ready-made markets. Although the product or service you would like to offer may be completely different from anything that has gone before, the chances are that it will be related directly or indirectly to a business which is firmly rooted.

By studying the past issues of magazines slanted to your proposed venture, you will notice advertisements which are regular to the point of being permanent. There are also those which appear for a month or two and then fade. It takes very little acumen to realize that the people who advertise regularly are offering something which the public want. If your product has any affinity to something that is being offered by these steady advertisers, you have a ready-made market.

Examples of industries which have grown around a ready-made market are all around you. The people who sell coffee, for instance, have created markets for coffee pots, thermostats, coffee filters, automatic percolators, store signs, coffee grinders and coffee vending machines; to mention just a few. Even such a widely advertised and everyday object as the cigarette has stimulated sales of ash trays, filter tips, cigarette lighters, apparatus for magicians to vanish or produce them, cigarette-making machines (both domestic and industrial), tobacco-curing sheds and packaging machines. The list is of course much, much longer, but all those satellite products had to be invented or sold by someone—and they had a market ready and waiting.

TODAY'S BIGGEST MONEY SPINNERS

The biggest sales items today are those which relate to the four top basic desires of mankind: food and drink, personal comfort, to appear attractive to the opposite sex, and the welfare of loved ones.

Food and drink are of course essential to life itself, but modern mankind has achieved such a variety of both food and drink that he has become selective in what he prefers to eat and drink. The American housewife is told by television that her children love breakfast cereal, her husband prefers a certain type of beer and she would find it difficult to maintain her health and vitality without taking her daily supplement of iron vitamins. All products and services associated with food and drink have a strong record of sales.

Personal comfort has been the driving force behind many inventions; even the wheel was a device to make it easier to transport heavy loads. Foam cushions, denture fixatives, arch supporters for the feet and hot water heaters are but a tiny fraction of the myriad of inventions and services supplied to the public every day to help maintain their comfort.

To appear attractive to the opposite sex is one of life's greatest driving forces. Any product or service which will successfully provide a person with even the slightest amount of sex appeal is a winner almost as soon as it appears on the market. This driving force accounts for the phenomenally successful after-shave lotions and colognes. It is the secret behind the sales of deodorants and it has done nothing to hurt the sales of toothpaste, cosmetics, wigs, clothing, perfume, hair dressings, soap, nail clippers, mirrors or shoe polish. Sauna baths, hair dressers, beauty salons and slimming courses all thrive on the individual need to appear attractive.

The welfare of loved ones has been responsible for the sales of fire warning systems, insurance and playpens. There are people who derive considerable income from drawing up wills and legacies, and there are others who specialize in providing service or products for children. Sanitized diaper service, tiny tot books, high chairs and disinfectant cleaners all stem from a desire to care for our loved ones.

Look around you for advertised items which fall into one of the four basic desire categories. Then make a survey of the average price of the goods sold in that category.

You may find for instance, that in the food and drink category the average selling price is about $4. The personal comfort item can run as high as an average of $50, not taking into account such items as automobiles which are more a necessity than a comfort.

These figures will give you a very accurate working guide to the price range in which you are most likely to be successful.

Your list is now almost complete, and you have before you an outline of all the information you need to make a decision which will have a profound effect on your future.

THE SWITCH FROM POSITIVE THINKING TO POSITIVE ACTION

By this time you are probably ready to start things moving. You have a good idea of the amount of time you can set aside and you have formed some decisions on the direction in which you would like to travel.

You'll have to decide whether your project is going to be a family affair or whether you're going to go it alone. Some people work best alone. They prefer to make any mistakes unseen.

Skepticism by a close member of the family can be very discouraging, especially in the early stages. If you have that type of family, then just go it alone and say nothing. Let the proof of your success be self-evident.

If your family works together in a spirit of helpful cooperation, then make plans which will form it into a tightly-knit organization with those involved putting forward their share of ideas and accepting some of the responsibility.

Once you have formulated the project, make a chart which can be hung on the wall. At the top of the chart, write the name of your program and the anticipated date of its completion. On the left side of the chart, list all the various stages through which your program has to go to completion, and alongside each stage, write the projected date for that part of the program. As each stage is completed, put down a check mark and the date it was completed.

You'll need a small area which can be used as an office or workshop. With every business there is the inevitable paperwork. Lost invoices or missing statements can mean loss of profits, so from the very beginning, be methodical. Schedule your day-to-day work, check that every stage of your venture is going according to plan and try to keep all your equipment, products and paperwork in orderly fashion.

Start meeting people who may be able to supply you with information on your project. There's no need to tell them why you need the information, but the more ideas and opinions you can obtain, the sounder your eventual decisions will be. When members of the family are working together, especially husband and wife teams, they can often contribute a specialized knowledge.

HOW TO MIX AND MATCH IDEAS INTO UNBELIEVABLE RICHES

Ted B. relaxed by making things. Nothing very large or elaborate, just helpful household gadgets. The sort of thing where upon walking into one of his rooms, the lights would turn on and the radio would begin to play.

His wife Eve is quiet and home loving. Cooking and dressmaking are her relaxation. They have two daughters; Suzy, aged ten and Pam, aged five.

Ted had just finished making an experimental shrink pack device and was looking for something on which to try it out. Eve had made two doll dresses from scraps of material for Pam. To Ted, they seemed ideal articles for shrink packaging—a way of placing products on a small card, covering them with clear plastic and passing them through a heat tunnel, causing the plastic to shrink and hold the articles firmly in place, ready for display.

The results were even better than he had expected and proved to have more far-reaching effects than he had imagined.

He brought his products in from the garage where he had been working on his small machine and showed them to Eve. "I was just thinking," he said, "You know that sofa that you are wanting? Well, I reckon that if you were to make a few of these and I was to shrink them on a decent bit of card, we'd sell them as easy as falling off a log."

Eve was doubtful, but the thought of a new sofa was a powerful incentive. "Well it's not going to cost us very much to try," she said, "I've got plenty of scrap material."

That was five years ago. They now have a business which produces more than 1,000 articles of doll's clothing every week. Dresses, coats, hats, swimwear and casuals are made in a variety of sizes at prices ranging from $1.25 to $2.95. They have even sold a few doll's fur coats made of genuine mink, and Eve not only has her new sofa, she has a new house in which to put it.

Combining two hobbies or recreational interests, will often result in the evolution of products that enjoy a steady sale.

Electronic technology and photography are responsible for a considerable number of products including enlarger timers, color analyzers and electronic flash units. Carpentry and rock collecting brought about black light showcases. Golf and electrical engineering gave us automatic indoor golf, and the man who devised the machine which sets up the pins on a bowling lane has probably never regretted his inventiveness.

Opportunities are everywhere. Your spare time can carry you to wealth and prosperity. Every day that passes is a day that can take you nearer to a life of comfort and security. Start now and put the cares and problems of financial worry behind you forever. There will never be a better time than now.

Chapter 2

How to Power Think Your Way to Wealth

There are many striking differences between the successful, wealthy person and the person who struggles through each day in a stifling atmosphere of frustrations and boredom. The most significant and obvious difference is the tremendously positive attitude of the successful individual.

To be successful in any field, you must possess a powerful, driving determination to succeed. Mental toughness is essential. Half-hearted decisions and lukewarm enthusiasm can defeat the most promising venture right from the very beginning. So, even before you begin formulating your spare-time project, know with absolute certainty that you are going to succeed. As your enthusiasm moves into top gear, you'll discover that there are dozens of people ready, willing and even well-paid to help you.

A THOUSAND DOLLARS' WORTH OF
INFORMATION—FREE

Within the four walls of your local library are thousands of dollars' worth of vital, accurate information. It's all yours for the taking.

Gordon W. saw some photographs of stained glass windows and became intrigued by the thought of depicting a sunrise scene on the large picture window of his mountain cabin.

His first step was to gather information on the types of dyes used and the methods of application. Gradually, his interest spread to the techniques of glass leading. Gordon experimented first on small pieces of glass and then on the smaller windows of his cabin before tackling the large picture window. As his knowledge and skill grew, neighbors asked him to decorate their cabin windows with hunting, woodland and angling scenes.

With the public library as his guide, Gordon W. began to explore the idea of producing kits for people who wanted to make their own stained glass windows. From the Directory of Manufacturers, he obtained names and addresses of firms able to supply him with raw materials at wholesale prices, and the telephone directory guided him to a local printer who was able to arrange for a simple book of instructions.

The librarian helped him to select several books which provided solid advice on the best methods of direct mail and mail order selling. Within six months of placing his first advertisement in one of the hobby and handicraft magazines, Gordon's monthly spare time income had grown to $800, equal to the income from his regular job. The $1,000 which he borrowed from his bank for his first batch of raw materials, packaging and printing, was repaid after four months.

Public libraries are able to provide information on almost every conceivable subject. They are at your disposal to assist you with up-to-date manufacturing and marketing methods. They will tell you where and how to buy materials, and can provide full details on every aspect of financing your project. This wealth of invaluable information is yours, completely free.

With this tremendous moneymaking information so readily available, you may pause to wonder why your local library is not jammed with people all seeking ways to increase their living capacity or expand their bank balance. The answer is what you might expect. Some people are content to sit back and wait for fortune to smile, while others set in motion a chain of events which seemingly creates wealth out of thin air. These people have learned the secret of attracting money.

HOW TO BECOME A HUMAN MONEY MAGNET

Jeff S. worked as a luggage supervisor at a large airport. He liked his job and he enjoyed meeting and talking with people. But like many other men who strive to get ahead, he was constantly seeking ways to achieve greater financial stability; to become independently wealthy. After many false starts, a conversation over a cup of coffee with a complete stranger put him on the right road to success.

"Turn yourself into a money magnet," the stranger told him. "Tell yourself that you are already moving towards a new and steady income. Act and think as if you are already wealthy. Decide how you will spend your money. Be alert to any and every opportunity, and you'll suddenly find them pouring down on you in a way you'd hardly believe."

For the next week, Jeff tried hard to convince himself that wealth was already moving towards him as if attracted by some mysterious cosmic force. He found himself thinking up schemes he would put in hand when wealth arrived and he began telling other people about his ideas.

During the second week, Jeff was offered the opportunity of taking over an office cleaning business. It was evening work, and the offer was made to him by a man whose regular job was

taking him to another part of the country. The man wanted
$2,000 for the spare-time business, but agreed that it could be
paid from Jeff's earnings over the next two years. Jeff decided
that it was too good an opportunity to refuse.

That same week he was offered a partnership in a cycle
repair business. A few days later he was offered the opportunity
to become the representative of a baggage manufacturing company. Just as he had been told, once things started to roll they
gathered tremendous momentum.

Today, four years later, with a spare-time income of over
$25,000 a year, Jeff still works as the supervisor. He still enjoys
the work, but his smile is serene and his job is almost of secondary importance. He has two teams of office cleaners working for him on routes he has established. He also acts as a field
agent for the baggage manufacturer and his latest interest is in
the buying and selling of silver bullion.

He says that there is never a week that passes without a new
opportunity for a spare-time income being offered to him. His
mind has become tuned to the tremendous wealth that is always
available to those who really want to achieve it.

TESTED METHODS OF SELECTING A
PROFITABLE VENTURE

All spare-time businesses have a small element of risk.
There is always a possibility that a new venture will fail. The
financial risks are minor because the need to maintain a steady
income on which to live is taken care of by the regular occupation; but there are a few other risks which must be taken into
consideration. One of the most important of these is the chance
of failure due to a poor choice of a spare-time venture.

Your choice of a spare-time business is largely determined
by your interests and knowledge of the field you intend to enter.

Within that field, there are certain tests which you can make to determine your chances of success.

1. Ask yourself if you are completely sold on the venture you have in mind. Does it attract you so compellingly that you're prepared to set aside many other pleasures while you develop this spare-time business?

2. If you intend to sell a product, either by mail or in person, is that product exclusively yours? The chances of success are greatly increased when you are six jumps ahead of any competitors.

3. Following along the previous test, if the project is a sales venture and you do have an exclusive product, are you absolutely certain you can get supplies without difficulty? Money is wasted on the promotion of a product when it becomes impossible to supply that product. It is a big advantage to be able to control the production of any article that you sell, especially if it is an exclusive. However, even when controlling every step, you still have to ensure a steady supply of the raw material.

4. If the product is not an exclusive, you must have a concrete reason why people will buy your product in preference to others on the market. Is it cheaper? Manufactured better? More reliable? Safer? More convenient? Only you can judge the potential worth of your product. If it is going into competition with similar products, it must have a substantial edge if it is going to be quickly successful.

5. If you intend to offer a product for sale through magazine advertising, have you checked back on the success of advertisements of similar products in that magazine? Successful products successfully advertised will run for months, and in many cases, for years. Any advertisements which are discontinued in a period of

less than one year should caution you to re-evaluate before investing too much time or money.

6. Have you tested your service or product on the consumer? Even if the product is exceptional in every respect, the consumer can sometimes reveal errors in judgment with regard to both the product and the promotion. A well known manufacturer of mouthwash recently entered the field of room spray disinfectants. With justifiable pride their name was prominent on the side of the spray cans.

After a great deal of money had been expended on production and promotion, someone realized that the famous name, so long associated with mouthwash, could possibly confuse the consumer into using the room disinfectant and deodorizer as a mouth spray. The product has since been put on the market under a slightly different name, but the repackaging costs were considerable.

Before investing money in large scale production and promotion, try your product on the ultimate user, the consumer.

7. Finally, but by no means the least important, ask youself if you are certain that the project is practical. The most clever and ingenious ideas are worthless if they can't be carried through. Make sure that you have enough spare time at your disposal to make the project possible. Don't rely too much on other people, other than members of your immediate family. No one has your interests quite so much at heart as you have.

Your search for products and services which can be turned into money-making ventures, is not restricted to your personal hobbies or interests. While it is perfectly true that those interests indicate that you have a special knowledge in those fields, there are countless other fields, many of which you have probably never before considered or even heard about. These fields can be very interesting and profitable.

YOUR DAILY MONEY FINDER

One of the greatest of values for money bargains is still the daily newspaper. Every day, in every city throughout the country, the daily newspaper brings the headline stories, gives views and comments on social and economic issues, and provides current information on the world of entertainment. The daily newspaper can also be your personal money finder.

Behind the scenes of those social activities, are openings for you to make money. The classified advertisements are a treasure house of big money opportunities. Even the news behind the headlines, read by millions of people, can provide ways for you to become a millionaire within a very few months. Hard to believe? Perhaps, but perfectly true nevertheless.

Stephen P. read the headlines. At that time they told of problems which were to affect every home in the country. The oil shortage was upon us. Stephen was 22 years old and knew very little about oil and gasoline, other than that without them the entire country would screech to a grinding stop.

He reasoned that if he could find a company with oil to sell, he would have no difficulty finding a buyer. The method he chose to look for oil was by telephone. First, Stephen had to ask questions about oil and how it was made available before he could even begin looking for someone with oil to sell. Most of his questions were treated with contempt or harsh humor, but his persistence paid off.

On his 625th telephone call, Stephen P. found a company that was prepared to sell him a small quantity of oil. Many of his previous contacts had told him that if he could find any oil, they would be very interested in buying from him. Well, now he had found oil. The trouble was he didn't have any money with which to buy it.

His solution was to have the buyer wire him the money as soon as the oil was delivered and Stephen, in turn, paid the seller in the same way as soon as he received payment.

For a while these arrangements worked very well, but he ran into the biggest problem of all when a petroleum company offered to sell him half a million dollars worth of petroleum. It was the chance he had been waiting for, but again he suffered the difficulty of raising the money. No one was prepared to support him with that amount of cash.

Stephen persisted. Eventually he found a bank which would advance the money if he could find a guarantor. The situation still seemed hopeless. Who would stand as guarantor for half a million dollars?

The answer suddenly became obvious. Stephen went to the company that was prepared to buy that amount of oil and asked them if they would sign against the loan. Within hours the deal was completed and Stephen was on his way to his first million.

Newspapers can be your first step towards a million. Look beneath the cover stories. Study the business pages. Watch the "buy and sell" advertisements in the classified pages. When people are active, they want something. Put yourself in the position of being able to fill those needs.

Take for example, the column on the sports page which tells about the local golfing tournament. Those people need golf balls, clubs, caddies, a couse on which to play—and that course makes its own demands—flags, refreshments and spectators. Even spectators have requirements.

If you ever suffer the frustration of being unable to conceive a product or service which will bring you a hefty second income, pick up your daily money finder. It can lead you directly to wealth and prosperity.

THE STAGGERING RESULTS OF THINK SESSIONS

Ideas are free. They come and go in the twinkling of an eye. Sometimes the really good ideas make such an impression that they remain and are acted upon. Other times, the very idea that could make you wealthy, comes to your mind at an inopportune moment, and by the time you can get around to acting on it, you have forgotten what it was.

The obvious answer is to keep a notebook handy. Never let a good idea escape because you were too busy to make a note. But what about those times when the well of ideas seems to have dried up? How can you tackle those frustrating times when it seems that brilliant brainwaves are a thing of the past?

The answer lies in specially pre-arranged think sessions. Find yourself a room or private place where you can be alone for a couple of hours. Take along some refershments and a tape recorder. Now start talking to yourself—or rather, to the tape recorder.

Don't pause to carefully formulate phrases, just tell the recorder the thoughts which run through your mind. Sometimes you may find it preferable to direct your thinking along specific lines. You may for instance, want to devise a way of producing and selling jewelry.

Talk to the tape recorder, state the difficulties and problems involved in obtaining the gems you would like to use, the workshop you would like to construct and the sales system you would like to develop.

At first, self-consciousness will make your thoughts and ideas seem trivial and unworkable. But as you persevere and forget about the tape recorder, your thought patterns will gradually assert themselves and ideas will begin to pour forth in a stream which will grow stronger and stronger with every think session.

Patricia B. had spent most of her married life being a wife and raising a family. Now she felt it was time to strike out and do something for herself. She wanted to fill her spare time with some interesting activity, and if she could also make money with that activity, she would be even more content. Into what activity could she direct her energy and spare time?

Pat sat down at her kitchen table with pencil, paper and a pocket tape recorder. For a while she jotted down ideas and talked to her tape recorder about projects she thought she would like to tackle. Gradually, her ideas crystallized.

Pat had always been attracted by the color, patterns and shapes that nature seemed to provide especially for her. The golden shades of autumn glinted from the sprays of sycamore and oak leaves that decorated her living room. In spring and summer there were always bunches of roses and daffodils. It was the beach, however, which attracted Pat most. The pounding surf and glistening rocks gave her a feeling of peace and contentment. As it turned out, they also gave her a considerable income.

Pat B. began making plaques from plaster of Paris cast in molds made by scooping holes in the sand. In the bottom of those hollows were placed rocks, shells and seaweed. When the plaster cast was removed from the sand, the pieces of decorative material remained firmly embedded in the casting.

At first, the plaster plaques were simply a room ornament, but friends began asking her to make plaques for them and a new business was born. Today Pat makes a variety of plaques using a new plaster composition which sets harder and faster than plaster of Paris. Her products are sold by the novelty stores in a large number of coastal towns. Although production is no longer carried out on the beach (rather, it is in a small factory), the decorative plaques still capture that fragment of nature people want to take into their homes, and Pat's fast growing industry is presently bringing her $2,000 a month.

HOW TO BE YOUR OWN EFFICIENCY EXPERT

One of the most difficult and challenging aspects of running your own spare-time business, is the difficulty most people experience in running the business at top efficiency. If you were a large business, you would probably call on the services of one of the firms which specialize in telling people how to run their business at full efficiency. When you are starting small, however, you have to be your own efficiency expert.

The best way to do this is to take a look at the methods the efficiency experts use and copy them. Here are seven ways of building your business along truly efficient lines.

1. Deal with your mail the day you receive it. Don't let bills and letters accumulate in an untidy pile. Answer the letters and pay the bills, remembering to claim any swift payment discounts. If you are unable to pay the bill immediately, place it in a special filing tray for attention at the earliest possbile moment.

2. Schedule your day's activities. Write your daily program on a chalk board, place the board on a wall where you will see it several times a day, then stick to your schedule.

3. Check all invoices and statements for accuracy. Pay special attention to your telephone bill. The dollars you save will surprise you.

4. If you have to travel and call on people, organize your route to avoid traveling over the same tracks twice. It is also a good idea to keep a log of your calls, mileage and gasoline costs. It's possible that your calls can cost you more than they earn, but when you are made aware that this situation exists, you can take steps to correct it.

5. If you have a stock of articles for sale, keep a running inventory. A simple see-at-a-glance record will prevent you from losing sales because you have run out of an item or because you had a requested item in stock but didn't know.

6. Determine the hours you intend to spend on your spare-time business and keep to them.

7. Get one project off the ground and running efficiently before starting a second. If the first project is obviously a failure, cut it off firmly and start afresh. You can waste considerable time, and sometimes money, trying to salvage a project simply because it seemed a good idea at the time, or perhaps to build your own ego. If you have a failure on your hands, kill it. If you have potential

success, develop it fully and then expand to your next
venture.

SPECIAL BUSINESSES THAT ARE LOW ON POPULARITY AND HIGH ON DOLLARS

There's an old saying in the north of England, "Where
there's muck, there's brass." In other words, where there's dirt
there's money.

This is true of many very profitable businesses which can be
successfully tackled on a spare-time basis. The secret is in seeking out those jobs which, for one reason or another, most people
are reluctant to tackle.

Don O. complained to the owner of a gas station that the restroom he had just used was in deplorable condition. He was told
that it was as much as the manager could do to keep pace with
car repairs and pumping gas, to be able to spare time to clean
the rest rooms.

To Don, a man looking for a way to earn money in his spare
time, it took only a few hours to figure out a way to turn this opportunity into a big money-making proposition. Within six
weeks, he was supplying an evening restroom cleaning service
to ten gas stations and charging them $25 for cleaning their rest-
rooms six days a week. It was a job that no one else really
wanted, and the gas station owners felt that it was worth $25 to
bring their business up to standard.

At the end of the year, Don had two men working for him on
a spare-time basis, each cleaning ten stations. He was paying
them $100 a week and retaining $150 from each for himself.

For a while Don was content with this arrangement, and
then he found a way to turn it into still larger money. Today, he
sets up a gas station cleaning route of about a dozen gas stations,
works it for a few months to get it established and then adver-
tises a spare-time business for sale. So far he has sold four
routes at $2,000 each and one for $1,500.

There are many opportunities for making money in jobs that most people consider unpleasant—cesspool maintenance, steer manure sales, rodent and insect extermination, diaper service and garage cleaning—to name just a few.

HOW TO BUILD A SINGLE IDEA INTO A MILLION DOLLARS

There are many ideas that have brought large sums of money to the people who not only originated the idea, but persevered in its acceptance. The valve on aerosol spray cans, the shredded plastic in which lettuce is offered for sale, hummingbird feeders, portable water purifiers, mosquito repellants and car waxes—even the common padlock and monkey wrench brought personal fortunes to the men who pioneered them.

Quite often, getting the idea and developing it into a marketable commodity are two problems which have to be considered separately. Assuming that you have developed a product which you think will sell, you now have to set about getting the public interested.

The easiest way, but not necessarily the best, is to place your idea in the hands of one of the organizations which specialize in the commercialization of other people's ideas. There is the danger of an unscrupulous firm stealing the idea, but most legitimate idea developers will treat the inventor fairly; although they naturally require payment for their efforts, usually in the form of a percentage of the proceeds from all sales.

The other alternative is to develop it yourself. This is not too difficult, but with the natural impatience that comes with the desire to see a new idea become successful, you may feel that it takes forever to see sales climbing.

The first step in the development of a product is to give it a name and description. Make this description as complete and detailed as possible, then send the information to yourself by registered mail. Put the envelope, now stamped with the date, in a safe place without opening the envelope.

You have to decide at this point whether you are going to go directly to the public via a magazine or newspaper advertisement, or whether you are going to sell to wholesalers. If you can interest wholesale dealers in your product you can save yourself a considerable amount of time as these people have well-established outlets, and, in many instances, a team of salesmen who continually call on these outlets to keep them informed of new developments.

Another way of establishing a line of distribution to the public is to approach firms which specialize in selling by mail order. These people issue annual catalogues and regular supplements. If you can interest them in your product they will arrange to have it illustrated and printed in their next mailing.

These methods of distribution assume that you can arrange to have your product manufactured. This is by far the most profitable method of idea development. If you are not in a position to arrange for the manufacture of your product, you are then compelled to go to a manufacturer and sell him the idea—either for a percentage of the sales or for a single cash payment.

Just one word of warning. Before you offer your idea to anyone, write first, telling them that you have an idea in which you are sure they will be interested. Do not describe your idea in detail, but offer full information against a letter from them stating that they will not make any use of information provided by you if, after 28 days consideration, they decide they are not interested.

Any worthwhile idea can be developed either personally or through a product development organization; but the whole essence of making a fortune from a single idea is in working only on those ideas which really have considerable possiblities and ignoring those attractive brain children which are really impracticable flights of the imagination. There are millions of people waiting for new ideas in every conceivable field. You have only to think of one truly acceptable idea and your bank manager has a new preferential customer.

Chapter 3

How to Establish A Regular Spare-Time Income

The money you earn in your spare time is money added to the income you receive from your regular work. This spare-time money can be a large amount, or it can be quite modest. It could be that your spare-time venture is one in which you engage from time to time, or one to which you turn only when extra cash is needed. In order to build a really substantial bank balance, however, your spare-time project should be a steady, consistent money spinner and one which will automatically pyramid your wealth.

Your choice of a spare-time project will be largely determined by your interest and experience, but in every field there are those areas which produce a steady, and often considerable flow of cash. These are the areas which have a High Replacment Rate (H.R.R.).

Food, gasoline, water and paper are typical H.R.R. products, but not all of us are sufficiently fortunate to own an oil well or paper mill, so we have to aim a trifle lower. We must be satisfied to make our million just a little slower and just a little more ingeniously. Rest assured, that million is out there waiting for you.

HOW TO BUY AND SELL AT A PROFIT

The secret skills of buying and selling may be summed up in just a few words. **Buy as cheaply as possible, and sell for as much as you can get.**

Before you can buy at a low price, there are three things you must know. First, what it is you intend to buy. Second, the current retail price of that item. Third, where to buy what you want.

Items high on the H.R.R.list are: paper or plastic drinking cups, paper plates, plastic garbage bags, matches, pencils and ball point pens, children's shoes and sandals, hosiery, and most cosmetic items such as razor blades, lipstick and hair spray. All of these are items which are bought to be used and then thrown away.

There are, of couse, hundreds of products which require continual replacement and you'll select those which appeal to you and are most convenient to your way of working.

Your next question should be, "How much should I pay for these products?" To this question, there is only one answer. You must buy at "give-away prices," prices which at present you may regard as unrealistic. You are about to discover, though, that it is possible to buy many commodities at ridiculously low prices, and this is something that anyone can do once they know where and how to buy.

First you must know the current retail prices; that is, the price that the public pays for the merchandise you are contemplating buying. Then you must find out the wholesale price; that is, the price that the dealer pays. At this time you should also find out whether the dealer buys directly from the manufacturer or whether he buys from a wholesaler. The usual practice is for the dealer to buy from a wholesaler. Very few dealers buy directly from the manufacturer.

It is well worth your while to trace the merchandise right back to its source. You will often find that even the wholesaler buys from an intermediary known as a "jobber." These jobbers earn a good living by representing several manufacturers, usually in a similar line of business.

This method of doing business is a convenient one for the wholesaler because instead of having to deal with 20 or 30 manufacturers and all the resulting paperwork, he simply deals with the one company.

You'll soon discover that when merchandise passes through several hands on its way from manufacturer to consumer, there is one inevitable end result and it is one which will work in your favor. Every person who handles the product, even if only indirectly, is going to make a profit. They all add on their profit percentage. An item which goes directly from manufacturer to consumer is considerably less expensive than one which goes through a chain of intermediaries.

So we will assume that you have traced the product back to its source and you know the price of it at each stage of its distribution. You will probably think that you now know the lowest price at which it can be bought. Not so. There are three ways in which you can buy at a still lower price.

1. Manufacturers' Job Lots. When a manufacturer changes his product or when a line is not selling very fast, the manufacturer will often offer the remainder of his stock at a very low price to a "job buyer" in order to clear it from his factory. He will do this to try to salvage some of his material costs and to make room for new products.

2. **Auctions.** Every big town has regular auctions at which the stock of businesses which have failed are sold by auction. These auctions are held so that creditors may recover some of the money which is owed to them. As a job buyer, you can often buy the merchandise you seek at a price well below the manufacturer's cost. Watch your newspapers for advertisements stating where and when auctions are to be held. They will also tell you the type of merchandise being offered. Many of the larger auctioneers send out regular bulletins to people on their mailing lists, giving details of forthcoming auctions. If you find this method of buying successful, you can ask to have your name added to the mailing list.

3. **Dealer's Surplus.** Almost every storekeeper overbuys at one time or another. Lines which have slowed or stopped selling gather dust on the shelves. If approached correctly, many shopkeepers will be ready to sell lines with which they are "stuck." They will try to recover as much of their cost as they can, but it is up to you to buy at the very lowest price. Here is a small piece of information which will help you.

Let's suppose a merchant buys some articles at $8 each, intending to sell them at $12 each. That would seem to represent a reasonable profit margin and we will imagine that he buys 20 such articles. At the end of the first week he has sold five, and there is $60 in his cash register. But things slow down and at the end of the month he has only sold another five. Six months later he has sold three more and there are seven more left to sell. Sales of that item have come to a standstill. There are several reasons why this may happen. It could be that the product sold initially because of extensive advertising by the manufacturer. It's also possible that a new and competitive product appeared on the market. Whatever the reason, until the storekeeper has sold at least one more of the original 20 articles, he has not made a penny profit. Those seven unsold articles are taking up expensive space which could be used for new merchandise which may sell faster.

If the merchant can be persuaded to sell you all those remaining seven articles for just $10, he has made $6 profit. True, he may not have made sufficient profit to cover his overhead, but the $6 in his hand is better than $56 worth of deteriorating merchandise sitting on a shelf—and you will have paid just under $1.50 each for them.

This takes you to your next step—selling. If you have bought at an attractive low price, you will have no difficulty selling what you have bought, regardless of what the merchandise is. In the previous example, you could sell those articles at $3 each and make 100 percent profit. However, it is obvious that if you have an article which was manufactured to sell at $12, you should have no difficulty in selling it at $6. You have only to sell two at this price and you have made a profit of $2. Every article you sell from then on is all profit.

Now that you have your product, bought at a very good price and are ready to sell it at a figure which will show you a handsome profit, your next step must be to find buyers for that product. You are already well aware of many of the avenues you can explore. Swap meets, newspaper classified advertising, door-to-door canvassing, sales parties, garage sales or even renting a small store on a month-to-month basis will put your product into the hands of the public. But all these opportunities need an extra push to keep them moving and that push can be supplied by a very powerful motivator called **publicity.**

PUBLICITY IDEAS THAT ATTRACT CUTOMERS

Until people know that you have something to sell, your sales figures are going to leave something to be desired. Even a whole page advertisement in a newspaper will have little effect unless there is something in that advertisement which will attract the public. So, getting back to basics, what does the public want? The answer includes wealth, health, social prestige, security, comfort and the like.

The publicity you arrange for your product need not cost you very much. In fact, there are ways of publicizing your business which will cost almost nothing at all.

Lew S. had gradually eased into the buying and selling business. He worked as a packer in a plastics factory Monday through Friday, and on Saturdays he called on stores to buy their surplus merchandise in small lots. At first, Lew sold this merchandise to other stores in a different part of town, content with a small profit. His first big step came when he was able to rent a small store at a very low rent in a poorer part of town. It provided him with space to store his merchandise and it had a window for display. His second big step came when he realized the power of publicity.

Lew S. had bought 1,500 tubes of hand cream for $500, or just over 33¢ each, directly from a manufacturer. In this instance, the creams were good quality with a suggested selling price of $2.49. The creams were not selling because they had come under competition from another manufacturer whose similar product was selling better because it was heavily perfumed. The manufacturer who was losing sales decided that his cream would have to be perfumed in order to compete.

Although Lew knew that he could sell them easily for 50¢ each, he decided to combine them with a previous buy and advertise them in a newspaper as a "housewives special." A few weeks before, Lew had bought a truckload of rubber matting offcuts. They measured 18 by 24 inches and they cost him 2¢ each. As they were too soft to use as doormats, he contemplated selling them as automobile floormats. His final idea, however, was a winner.

He ran a small advertisement in the local newspaper, advertising the hand cream for 99¢ and offering free with purchase a "feet saver" rubber mat to be placed in front of the kitchen sink to help the housewife alleviate tired feet. He sold his entire stock of hand cream in two weeks.

Building ideas to attract customers can be an interesting challenge. The secret is to concentrate on those basic human needs. Study the advertising in a dozen different magazines and you'll soon discover that the successful advertisers, those that run full page advertisements month after month and year after year, almost invariably slant their advertisements directly at one of those basic human needs. Follow their example. Anything that you want to sell can be tied directly or indirectly to this method of attracting customers.

There are very few spare-time enterprises that will not show an immediate and impressive response as a result of advertising and publicity.

Advertising is generally understood to mean the dissemination of a message by means of radio, television, newspapers, magazines, or direct mail. Publicity is rarely quite so dignified. Publicity is the blast from a trumpet, the shouting from a rooftop. Publicity can be hilariously funny or shockingly dramatic, and publicity can be another of your steps to a spare-time fortune.

HOW TO GET AS MUCH PUBLICITY AS YOU COULD POSSIBLY WANT

Successful publicity is the result of careful, calculated planning. The original concept may come to you as a blinding flash of inspiration, but the execution of the idea will only produce top results when it has been the subject of considerable thought. Your mind can be a powerhouse of inventiveness, more capable of producing ideas than the most complex computer ever built. Put that powerhouse to work!

First is the idea. You need a method of making the public sit up and take notice. You want to be talked about and, if possible, you want an idea which will attract the attention of the news media.

Ronald Gaddie of North American Bait Farms, Inc. is a man of ideas. He has pushed his business from a backyard enterprise to a million dollar business. Whenever things looked as if they may be slowing down, Ronald was ready with an idea which would provide his business with the required stimulus.

His most recent idea was sufficiently startling to warrant Channel 7 Eyewitness News sending a reporter and camera crew to the bait farm. That evening, television viewers were astounded to watch Ronald Gaddie eating worms. "They're very nourishing," he explained, "almost entirely protein, and when prepared properly can make really good eating." He then proceeded to give a short cookery demonstration which was followed by the announcement that North American Bait Farms was going to hold a competition for the best recipe using worms as the main ingredient. The top prize was to be $500 and the only stipulation was that the winner would have to help eat the prepared food.

A woman in St. Paul, Minnesota was the winner in the competition; but even if there had never been a single entry, the publicity achieved was considerable.

The ideas for a publicity stunt are never in short supply. They can be small, modest schemes restricted to the local area, or they can be bombshells which thunder across the nation.

Ray T. works as a furniture salesman during the day, but his six month old electronics repair business brings him almost as much money from the work he does in the evenings. Ray recently arranged for the public library to hold an exhibition of sound activated burglar alarms. He chose the public library partly because he knew it would intrigue the young people, and partly because he thought it might bring him a little publicity.

He certainly wasn't prepared for the tremendous avalanche of orders which poured in on him. Within the first week he had received 25 orders ranging in value from $250 to $1,500. The orders came from stores and industries requesting that their premises be burglar-proofed with his electronic gadgetry. Ray T. is now slanting his spare-time business towards the new opportunities in security and burglar protection.

The motion picture business has always been publicity minded, and many new films have been released to a nationwide surge of publicity and fanfare. Even the private individual sometimes hits national headlines—people that have elected to walk from New York to Los Angeles or bicycle round the world. Men have flown under the span of London Bridge or climbed to the top of Eiffel Tower.

Publicity stunts do not always require the daredevil approach; they can be as simple as something contrived in your own backyard. The only condition which must be fulfilled for a publicty stunt to be really successful is that it must be considered newsworthy.

When the idea begins to formulate in your mind, you should take into consideration the day and time at which it will take place. Newspapers, radio and television should be informed as far ahead as possible, so that if they are interested (and they will be if your publicity stunt is sufficiently startling), they may arrange to give full coverage.

Probably one of the simplest and most effective ways to publicize your new business is by means of a news release. This is a concise, informative statement about your new business or an interesting development of an established business. The release is typed double-spaced with a pertinent heading and should give all the essential information without flowery overwriting. It should then be duplicated and sent to all the local newspapers and radio stations. Most newspapers are interested in gathering information about items which could affect their readers. If they judge your particular project to be of sufficient communal interest, they will either print the release very much as it was sent to them or, if it is extra newsworthy, they may send a reporter to gather further information. A news release which is accompanied by an illustrative photograph stands a slightly better chance of attracting the editor's attention than one which is simply a written report.

Successful publicity will bring customers flocking to your door or will make it possible for you to receive a welcome reception at theirs. However, this is only part of the way to your first million. The next step is knowing how to take full advantage of that publicity. Having gotten one foot in the door and having successfully gained the interest of your potential customer, you now have the task of convincing them that they really need the product or service you offer. In other words, you have to know how to sell.

SECRETS OF SUCCESSFUL SELLING

If the product or service you are offering is a high demand item, one that people already know they want, your task of selling is considerably easier. Even with this advantage, though, there are several tricks in selling which can make the difference between a large profit or, in some cases, no profit at all.

They are simple tricks based on psychology and are in the handbook of every company salesman. They should be part of your way of life because if you are going to make a great deal of money, you are going to do it by selling. No matter what your product or service, you have got to sell somebody something; even if it is only an idea. So read, think about and act on the following suggestions. They could be the most important words you will ever read. Learn how to acquire irresistible sales dynamics.

1. **Know Your Product.** It is much easier to sell an article or service with which you are completely familiar than it is

to sell something about which you are unsure. It is safe to assume that if you are inventing or manufacturing a product, you will know just about everything there is to know about it. But when you are buying to resell, take time out to learn everything there is to know about what you have to offer.

2. Have Faith in Your Product. When you know beyond any doubt that what you are selling is the prettiest, the safest, the most durable, the biggest, the smallest, etc., your certainty comes across in your selling. If you are convinced that your product is exactly what you claim it to be, your voice carries a tone of authority—and people listen.

Go into a store and meet a salesman who has secret reservations about one of the products he is selling. You will know instantly that things are not quite what they should be and it will take more than advertising claims or a low price to sell you that product.

3. Limit The Choice. When a customer is hesitating, trying to make a final choice, don't confuse the issue by suggesting further alternatives. Take the reverse action. Try to help your customer narrow the choice. Logically, if you can limit the choice to two items and then find a good reason to remove one of them, the customer will then buy the remaining item.

Let us imagine that you are selling homemade jewelry and although you originally showed about 20 pieces, your customer is undecided between a gold ring with a red stone and a silver ring with a diamond.

Remove all other pieces and leave the customer just the two from which to make the choice. If the customer is really undecided, there is a good possibility that he or she will buy both pieces if price is no barrier. But it is more probable that their mind is already made up and they just need a little push in the right direction. At this time bring into action the "Give them what they want" technique.

4. Give Them What They Want. One of the greatest secrets of being a good salesman is in listening to what the customer says. Too often the salesman, full of enthusiasm for his product, will reel off a list of good features regardless of whether or not the customer is interested in those particular features.

Although the following instance is somewhat exaggerated, it doesn't wander too far from many true examples of poor sales techniques.

A man walks into a television store and says he is interested in a color set with a 21-inch screen at a reasonable price. The salesman immediately leads the way to a magnificent set in the center of the showroom.

"This is the latest color set from XYZ, one of the oldest manufacturers in the business. It incorporates magic eye centrifugal tuning, a distortion free 25-inch screen, triple woofer speakers and simplex color differentials. One of the finest televisions on the market, and this week we have it on special, reduced from $1,200 to $900."

A fine television it may be, but until the salesman shows the customer a reasonably priced set with a 21-inch screen, he is in danger of losing the customer's confidence. Of course it is possible that the salesman can point out the superior features of a bigger or better television and upgrade the sale, but that should come after showing the customer what he wants to see. The customer with definite preferences usually has a firm reason for those preferences.

There are times when the customer is cautious. He wants to hear all the pros and cons of all the products being offered, but a good salesman will quickly detect the selling points which are the major interest of the customer simply by listening. Questions such as, "Does this one have a . . . . . . ?" or "Which are the models with a built-in safety device?" give the game away to an alert salesman. Follow the well-beaten path of the super salesmen and listen to your customers.

5. Sell The Benefits. There is an old advertising adage which says, "Don't sell the bacon, sell the sizzle." There are many products in which the customer has no real interest. The only thing they really want to know is "Will it do what I want it to?" or "Will it give me the results for which I am looking?"

The housewife is not too concerned with the granularity or color of her new laundry detergent. All she really wants to know is if it will get her clothes cleaner. The motorist doesn't really care if the new motor oil smells like roses or carnations, but he is intensely interested in knowing how much it will improve engine performance.

So whatever you have to sell, whether it is a service or a product, make sure your customer knows that what you are offering will provide him with the **benefits** he wants.

6. **Have Faith In Your Product.** Any insincerity on your behalf will send warning signals at a subconscious level to your potential customer. A discerning customer can detect falseness instantly.

All of the foregoing tricks of irresistible sales dynamics will give you the edge over most of your competitors. They will help you make the sale and they will help you make it quicker. After all, time is expensive and it is **your** time and **your** money we are talking about.

SURE WAYS TO SAFEGUARD YOUR MOST VALUABLE ASSET

The more you earn, the more valuable each hour of your day becomes. It is of vital importance thay you guard each minute as if it were actually hard cash.

Joan L. had worked as a copywriter in an advertising agency for four years. She was constantly aware of the time lost every day by the need to take advertising copy to the typesetter and the inevitable amount of time expended in collecting the finished work. Although mailing the work saved office time, the total time taken for the work to be returned was too long. Hand delivery seemed to be the best answer to an aggravating problem inherent in the advertising business. It was on one particularly frustrating day, when an unexpected work load necessitated three successive trips to the typesetter, that Joan decided to drop out of full time copywriting and work part time while she established a pickup and delivery service for advertising agencies.

Joan L. calculated the time lost by the average advertising agency in delivering copy. She converted that time into an approximation of the amount of cash each trip cost the agency and decided that if she could persuade the agencies to let her take and deliver the work on a contract basis, she could cut a sizable amount from the agency's costs and still make a resonable income for herself.

First, Joan had to make sure that her service would be fast and dependable. She paid a visit to a number of typesetters until she found one who could provide her with consistent quality and firm delivery times in return for all the work she could get.

Within a year, Joan was working at her new venture full time and ran a small fleet of delivery vans with three young women working for her, all dressed in distinctive uniforms. Advertising agencies are quickly turning to her speedy and efficient service, saving themselves time and money while she is building a substantial and very profitable business. All of this is based on the fact that time is expensive.

If you are going to take those spare-time steps to your first million, there is one unremitting precept that you must never forget. **The more you earn, the more money your time is worth.** So many people who start working for themselves in their spare time seem to regard their time as being of no value. They compute their cost, their overheads, their income and their profit, but they forget to take into account the cost of their time.

If your spare-time venture takes 40 hours of your time every week and you are showing a profit of $400 per week, your time is worth $10 an hour, and this is precisely how much you stand to lose whenever you needlessly waste time. It is not a constant figure because as you become more efficient, your profit figure and your hourly rate increase. If you waste too much time when you could be earning, your profit will steadily decline.

From this moment on, start safeguarding your most valuable asset—your spare time. Draw up a schedule of the things you have to do and then do them (if you don't do them, you've wasted time drawing up the schedule). Avoid making trips or forming a sales route which takes you over the same territory twice when an alternative route would serve you better.

Try using the telephone to help you save time. Work it out for yourself. Which is more expensive, a telephone call or your hourly rate? Careful planning and forethought will help you put your business on a very firm foundation. If you set a guard against wasting irretrievable minutes, there will come a time when someone will say to you, "How lucky you are to have such a good second income." But is it luck or is it the result of astute thinking and a burning ambition to be wealthy?

HOW TO MAKE YOUR OWN GOOD LUCK

There are times when it seems that the winds of fortune definitely blow in our direction. Everything goes right, everything falls neatly into place. And there are times when we blunder from one catastrophe to another.

Good luck, bad luck. Some people attribute it to the astrological influences being right or wrong on certain occasions. Or perhaps it was that black cat this morning, or someone spilling the salt, forgetting to knock on wood or maybe seeing the new moon through glass.

We seem to find it easy enough to find reasons for being lucky or unlucky, but why shouldn't we make our own good luck? Why do we have to suffer the whims of chance? We don't. Here's a way to give people reason to put the word "Lucky" in front of your first name.

Let us assume we are all going to be granted our fair share of good luck and bad luck. This would mean that with all things averaging out according to the natural laws of the universe, any further good luck we make for ourselves has to throw the balance in our favor. So let's get started in the good luck business. At least, that's what other people would term it. We know it is really the outcome of a little shrewd thinking.

Luck is making the right contacts. Whatever you need, whether it's money, advice, opportunity, services or any other form of assistance to help you on your way to your first million, it is often available to you if you go out there and meet the right people.

How do we meet the right people? Simply by being sociable and friendly. Any of the people you meet every day could be the very person to help you, providing they know you need help. If they cannot help personally, there's a good chance they'll know someone who can. Give them the opportunity. Ask their advice about problems that are proving a stumbling block in your efforts to succeed. People are always pleased to be asked for their advice and it seems a rule that the more successful the person, the more willing they are to provide you with assistance. After all, when you are successful and meet someone who is struggling at the bottom of the ladder, aren't you going to help them up a rung or two? Aren't you going to remember your own earlier problems and know how you can help this person get started?

But don't just be content with making efforts to meet people who can help you. Take every step to help yourself. Keep informed. Take every opportunity to pick up a current magazine or newspaper and read. Before you go to sleep every night, try to find 10 or 20 minutes in which to work your way through a book dealing with a subject in which you are interested.

Keep abreast of both the local and international news. You will be amazed at the way in which the information you gather proves useful to you in your spare-time business. It seems that like attracts like. If you break a leg you'll probably meet one of your friends hobbling around on crutches. A famous film star dies, another follows in a few days.

Luck is being in the right place at the right time. If you follow the local news and make yourself aware of forthcoming events, and if you keep yourself informed of the interesting developments which are constantly taking place around you, being in the right place at the right time is not too difficult.

Friends might say "You were lucky to be on hand when that corporation started looking for your special type of service," or "How lucky you happened to have a stock of those new electronic fire warning devices just when the city council decided to recommend their use." How lucky? Not luck at all— just foresight. Perhaps there's no such thing as luck, although John N. might be inclined to disagree.

John grows four-leaf clovers. He started selling the clover embedded in heart-shaped plastic pendants. Gradually, he expanded his business and now his four-leaf clovers may be found decorating a multitude of items from resin-topped patio tables to ash trays, and paper weights to plastic-covered kitchen counter tops.

John N. believes in good luck, with a gross income of over $30,000 a year; but perhaps he, too, made his own opportunities. Good luck can also be having the necessary cash ready when a bargain is offered.

SYSTEMS OF FINANCE BUILDING

If your spare-time business is to provide you with a regular source of income, the finances must be sound. The first step in ensuring a solid foundation is to accurately assess your capital.

As a spare-time venture, your business does not necessarily need a hefty financial backing. With a regular source of income to pay your rent and put food on the table, the spare-time business can often be started with a minimum of capital. However, it really depends on the type of business you are contemplating.

For example, if you decide to start a spare-time business as a soil consultant, your initial investment may be a simple soil test kit and perhaps a microscope. If you intend to use your knowledge of plastics to produce a new type of child's toy, you are faced with placing production in the hands of a plastics molding company or investing considerable money in compressors, cooling tanks, injection equipment and raw material.

Most spare-time businesses require very little capital. It is one of the greatest advantages of the spare-time business. But even with the minimum requirements, you will need a little cash for advertising, travel, printing, postage and all the usual expenses incurred by every type of business. Decide how much cash can be budgeted as capital and use this as the basis of your projected income.

The next figure you need to know is that of your costs. This is the amount of money needed to buy supplies and equipment and all the inevitable overhead expenses including printing, telephone, electricity, postage and advertising.

Base all your cost calculations on the assumption that business is going to be at a low ebb at first. A new business rarely gets off the ground with a big influx of profit. You should expect to grow at a steady rate, but if your cost calculations are conservative, you will probably end your first six months agreeably surprised.

When your business can be seen to have a steady growth, you may decide to expand slightly. This step may take the form of more extensive advertising or the purchase of automatic equipment to take the place of the manual equipment you bought to get started. At this time you will discover that capital is easy to acquire. Banks and private lenders are much more interested in helping to finance a business which has proved itself to be successful than they are in the pipe dream of an untried venture.

When your business is established and running smoothly, your credit will be in good standing. Manufacturers of equipment will usually be agreeable to split the cost of your purchase, spreading it over a few months, interest-free.

It is when you reach the stage of expansion that you may wish to consider the choice between enlarging your present business or venturing into another, possibly entirely different type of business. This type of expansion is know as diversification and has the advantage of removing some of the eggs from one basket. But it also has its dangers.

HOW TO DIVERSIFY SAFELY

Although diversification has several advantages, it can only be undertaken when the first business is firmly established. If you begin a second business and the first business fails because you were concentrating too much on the new venture, you are merely exchanging one business for another.

While the first business is growing, it needs all the force and drive you can give it. However, when it is running smoothly and all the difficulties encountered by a new business have been ironed out, you can begin investigating the possibility of another business.

The best type of diversification is in starting a second business which complements the first venture. Bill R. began remodeling kitchens in his spare time. He would start by pulling out all the old style cabinets and rebuilding with new ones styled along modernistic lines, featuring interior lights, turntables and fitted compartments.

The demand for the custom designed cabinets became too great for him to build them individually, and he began contemplating expanding his business by renting a small building and equipping it with modern cabinet-making equipment.

The advantages of automated cabinet manufacturing were obvious. Production would be fast, cabinets would all be to the new styling and he calculated it would take him about two years to recover the cost of his investment.

At this time, a friend to whom he had mentioned his intentions, told him about a manufacturer of hi-fi cabinets who was about to sell his equipment and retire. Two months later, Bill R. was the new owner of a small factory that made hi-fi stereo cabinets. Not only was he now in the hi-fi business with two part time employees, but the machinery which made the hi-fi cabinets was exactly what he needed for making his kitchen cabinets. The two businesses enable him to enjoy a personal income of $30,000 a year and he says that this is only the first step on his journey to financial independence.

Diversify only when you are sufficiently established to do so safely. Don't invest cash in a new venture at a time when the first business may be placed in jeopardy through insufficient funds.

It is very difficult to estimate the time it would take for a business to become established. A lot would depend on the type of business and the amount of time you can devote to it. One of the fastest-growing businesses which is extremely congenial, covering almost every conceivable product and which would probably attract more people into a spare-time venture than any other type of business, is mail order.

Chapter 4

How to Mail Your Way to a Fortune

Of all the different types of ventures you may consider en route to your first million, mail order must surely be the ideal spare-time venture. The starting capital requirements are quite small, you are completely free to select the working periods which are most suitable to you, your choice of merchandise or service is virtually unlimited, and because you rarely see the people to whom you sell, your "office" could well be your living room or garage. You are about to discover how to become a master of mail order.

Although the term **mail order** is usually applied to any business which uses the U.S. Mail Service to receive and fulfill orders, for the sake of convenience we will make a distinction between mail order and direct mail.

Mail order will be considered to be the placing of advertising in newspapers and magazines. Direct mail, which will be covered in the next chapter, will be considered as a business conducted by sending advertising material directly to the potential customer.

HOW TO GET STARTED

To get started in mail order, you will need a minimum of office equipment. A typewriter, two or three ledgers, a filing system (which could be as simple as a cardboard box), some headed letter paper and some envelopes are necessary. You will probably need labels and packing material if your product requires them.

You will also need sufficient capital to run your advertisement in at least six issues of the magazine or newspaper which you decide is the most suitable for what you have to offer. Your final and most important requirement is a cash-pulling product or service.

All this sounds very simple and straightforward; requirements that are easily met. And so they are, but let's look into it a bit closer and you'll soon discover that a little knowledge can save you a whole pile of disappointments and wasted time.

The typewriter. A new electric model would be sheer luxury, but an old, well-used manual typewriter will serve just as well. All you need is one that is legible and reliable. If you are pinching pennies, leave the more expensive items until the cash starts coming in.

The headed letter paper. This is part of your shop window. The people who are going to be potential customers may never meet you or know for sure whether you are a one man business working from a corner of your living room, or a large, well-staffed company operating from a magnificent suite of offices.

Your advertisements, your letter, the product and possibly a brochure, are all your customers have on which to form an opinion of your business.

With this important thought in mind, your letterhead should be attractive and businesslike. It may be worth your while to have a professional design artist prepare your letterhead for you. The cost would be minor compared with the favorable impression created by a professional looking letterhead.

At this point you should also consider the name you are going to use, and if it is not your own, register it under the Fictitious Names Act.

THE SIX ISSUES OF THE MAGAZINE OR NEWSPAPER YOU SELECT

Here we run into the first of the major decisions. Why six issues? You could very well strike gold the first day your advertisement appears, in which case you would want to continue the advertisement and at the same time be blessed with the happy knowledge that it was already paying for itself. If it does not pull too well on the first issue, you must be prepared to give it a fair chance by continuing with it before contemplating a change. Later in the chapter we will explore the different types of media most suitable for mail order advertising.

Now we come to the final and probably most important decision ever to be made in mail order. The choice of product or service. Where does one find a million dollar product? How would you even know a money spinner if you saw it?

E. Joseph Cossman, one of the kings of mail order, will tell you that he saw an advertisement in the Business Opportunities section of the **Los Angeles Times**, offering a fly killer in the form of a doughnut-shaped insecticide.

With good promotion, Joe Cossman's company sold over two million Flycakes in the first year. The Flycake fulfilled four of the basic human needs. Comfort, freedom from fear and danger (disease), welfare of loved ones and cleanliness. Any product which effectively exterminates flies will always have universal acceptance.

Watch your newspapers, trade magazines and trade shows for news of new products. Contact local manufacturers, and even if they are not personally involved in the manufacture of a new product, it is very likely that they will be aware of new developments in their trade. Try placing your own advertisement asking for information on new ideas or inventions.

Mary S. placed an advertisement in a major newspaper requesting information on new products. Within a week she had 42 replies, and the one which interested her the most was a shampoo for pets.

It came in the form of a thick, syrupy liquid, pleasantly perfumed, and it cost $2 for a four oz. sachet. Each sachet diluted down to 20 gallons of working solution. Mary checked through the yellow pages of her telephone directory for a manufacturer of plastic bottles until she found one who was prepared to supply her in small quantities. The cost of the bottles in the one pint size was 4¢ each, complete with screw cap.

A local printer supplied her with self-adhesive labels in two colors for $20 per 1,000. The labels, lavender and dark blue, described the contents as Superior Pet Shampoo, gave brief instructions for use and showed the price as $2.50 per 16 oz. bottle.

Mary then placed a small display advertisement in the Sunday supplement of the same newspaper which had produced the original response. The advertising cost her $125, and on its first appearance brought her 45 replies. On its second appearance she received 210 requests for the pet shampoo, and subsequent advertising settled to an average of 160 replies a week.

After 18 months, Mary S. had advertisements running in two Sunday supplements, a monthly pet magazine and a trade journal. The shampoo is still the major item in her catalogue which now includes 15 products and brings her a monthly spare-time income in excess of $4,000.

HOW TO FIND PRODUCTS WITH REAL APPEAL

Why do people buy by mail? Why do people carefully clip a coupon from a magazine, mail it to a firm of which they may never have heard before, and then wait trustfully and patiently for the mailman to bring the reply? There are a number of reasons and you should know some of them if you are going to succeed in the mail order business.

The public generally places a great deal of trust in the magazines and newspapers they read. They trust that the advertisements appearing on those pages are bona fide. They know that no publication would knowingly support a fraudulent enterprise. It follows, then, that they also expect the merchandise they order to follow very closely to the description in the advertisement.

There is also the convenience of shopping by mail. By walking as far as the mailbox, people can buy anything from a rubber stamp to a diamond necklace, or from a packet of flower seeds to a greenhouse filled with rare orchids.

For some people it is the element of anticipation and surprise that provides the attraction of shopping by mail. Then there is the implied or written guarantee that if the merchandise does not fully satisfy the customer, money will be refunded immediately with no questions asked. This feature is one of the most important facts of mail order and one you must constantly keep in mind.

Finally, there is the strongest reason of all for buying through mail order. It is that many of the items to be bought through mail order are unobtainable in any other way. This is the clincher.

You must find a product that people need to buy or feel that it would give them pleasure to own, and it should be a product which only you can provide.

It's fair to say that no matter how exclusive your product is if it's successful it won't be long before there is a competitive item being advertised in the same magazine. This, after all, is the basis of free enterprise. It may even be the way you got started.

Go to your public library and obtain about a dozen copies of magazines which cover the field in which you are interested. Go back a couple of years, if possible. Now look through the advertisements and make a note of those which appear month after month and year after year.

Remember that the people who are placing those advertisements are paying money to do so. They are not philanthropists and if those ads were not producing a profit, they would not be there.

So now you know the type of product which sells in your field of interest and this knowledge gives you a reasonable foundation on which to assess your chances of success. You need a product, possibly similar to those proven successful, and one which will fulfill certain requirements. It must fill one or more of the basic human needs and, preferably, it must be exclusively your own.

Where do you find such products? There are trade journals to cover every section of our way of life. Select the field which interests you and read the magazines which are directed at your special interests. Study the sections which deal with new products. Read the advertisements that seek representatives for new items. Watch for news of products presently being developed. With the information you will have gathered, certain products will suggest themselves to you as being likely items for mail order. Write to the manufacturer of those products, telling them of your interest and how you would like to market their goods. Providing they are agreeable, ask if they would send you information on their terms of business.

Another method of seeking new products is to apply to the Trade Department of foreign consulates. Many countries produce a monthly bulletin which gives information on a long list of products, all of which are seeking exposure and fresh markets. Trade shows are another good source for new products, as are the lists of government patents of products released for general manufacture.

Sometimes it is only a matter of giving a new twist to a once popular product. Dragging a box along the ground was fine until someone discovered how much easier it was when the box was mounted on wheels. Turn your brain loose and "put wheels on-to" products no longer in vogue.

It has been known for many years that cobalt chloride changes color from blue to pink as it absorbs moisture from the air, and then back to blue again as it dries out.

Darryl A. had an idea for "putting wheels on" an old piece of knowledge. He had a quantity of small pictures printed. One set featured a young Dutch girl with a bouquet of tulips and a windmill in the background. The other set showed a young Dutch boy with a toy sailing boat under his arm and a lake surrounded by banks of tulips in the background.

Darryl pasted the pictures onto small wooden plaques and then made small pleated skirts from crepe paper for the girls and a pair of baggy pants made from similar material for the boy. The pants and skirts were then dipped into a concentrated solution of cobalt chloride and left to dry. When they were completely dry, he pasted them into the proper position on the respective pictures.

His mail order idea pays off to the tune of over $800 a month. The weather watching boy and girl with clothes that change color with the changes in humidity was an instant success. Darryl had been doubly smart in manufacturing both a boy and a girl because almost invariably his customers bought one of each.

A mail order business is pleasant and interesting. It offers a challenge to your inventiveness and provides you with the opportunity to plan for the future. Even your advertising can be pre-tested to enable you to get the biggest returns for your dollar.

PRE-CALCULATING ADVERTISING MEDIA EFFECTIVENESS

Every dollar you spend on advertising must return its share of profit. In mail order where the entire business is based on the pulling power of your advertisement, it is doubly important to make sure that your advertising does its job properly. There are several ways in which your advertising can be evaluated, sometimes before you even spend a penny.

Before placing your mail order advertisement in a magazine or newspaper, there are a few things you must take into consideration.

1. You must choose the magazine or newspaper which will carry your advertisement. Your choice will be largely determined by your product. It would be a waste of money to place an advertisement for a power drill attachment in a women's fashion magazine. To help you determine the type of magazine most suitable for your purpose, select those which are already carrying advertisements for products or services similar to those you wish to offer.

Some novices, fearing the competition of established mail order firms, make the mistake of selecting a medium which merely reaches the fringe of the readers they really should contact. While it is true they face little or no competition, and they will probably get some replies; the results will not compare with the success which is possible by ploughing the more fertile fields of a correctly assessed readership.

2. Having selected the type of magazines, your next objective is to get as much exposure as possible for every dollar

spent. You can calculate this quite simply, and by doing so give yourself a very accurate guide as to the least expensive way to proceed.

To obtain a comparative cost of advertising in several magazines, write to the magazines which interest you, asking them for their advertising rate card and readership survey.

The rate card will give you a comparative figure for a full page advertisement. For instance, one magazine may quote $500 for a full page advertisement, while a comparative magazine may quote $350.

It would appear that the second magazine is the least expensive. But now you have a second set of figures to assess. From the readership survey, take the total circulation figure. You may be surprised to discover that the first magazine has a circulation of 1,500,000, while the second magazine reaches only 500,000. In this instance, it is obvious that the first magazine offers by far the better value for the money.

You can obtain the comparative figure by dividing the cost of a full page advertisement by the number of readers. This will tell you exactly how much it costs you to reach each reader with a full page advertisement. The same calculations apply to every size advertisement right down to the classifieds.

3. The readership survey will also give you another set of truly interesting figures. It will tell you exactly who reads the magazine. It will tell you by giving you information on the income, occupation, age group, hobbies and sex of its readers. It will probably even tell you the type of houses and specific areas in which these readers live. Where else could you get such valuable information, free? It lines up your target for you with an accuracy that has cost the magazine publisher thousands of dollars. He wants your advertising, but he also wants it to pay you back with big dividends. If it does, he knows you will grow—and so will your advertising budget.

Having determined the magazine or newspaper in which you are going to run your advertisement, there is one more step you can take to ensure its success. You can make your advertisements irresistible.

HOW TO WRITE EYE-CATCHING ADS

Once again, follow in the steps of the leaders. Study examples of advertising in all types of magazines. Watch for those ads which have been running for many months or even years, and it will quickly become apparent that each of them follows one of four easily identified patterns.

1. The word **you** is featured prominently. People are always interested in themselves and anything which concerns them attracts their attention.

2. It features a photograph or drawing which sets out to prove that the product or service supplies one or more of the basic human needs. That automobile polish gives a protective shine without hard work. It demonstrates comfort and prestige. The man holding a fistful of dollar bills to prove that XYZ carpet company can save you money displays economy and efficiency.

3. Fulfillment of one or more of the basic human needs is stressed in the advertising copy.

You can be more attractive to the opposite sex by using XYZ toothpaste.

You can be more comfortable in handmade shoes—beds—armchairs—etc.

You can be the envy of your neighbor by catching more fish—being able to play the piano—owning a swimming pool—etc.

4. The advertising copy is easy to read. The sentences are short and the words are common, everyday words.

So there you have it in a nutshell. If you want your advertising to produce results, appeal directly to the people whom you consider to be your potential customers and do so in a way which leaves them no room for doubt. Tell them about your product or service, but tell them in a way which is easily acceptable; even if it is only a small advertisement.

If you can afford to take a full page advertisement, you have room in which to give considerable information about what it is you have to offer. If you catch the reader's attention at the top of the page, he or she will continue to read the rest of the advertisement, **but only if you catch their attention in the first place.** What catches their attention? One of the four established attention grabbers you have just read.

There is one other feature used by some advertisers and it is something you may wish to try. It is the clip-out coupon. Sometimes a small coupon will spark a response simply because many people can't be bothered to sit down and write a short letter. With a coupon, all they have to do is fill in their name and address and place it in an envelope.

Making money in mail order is one of those spare-time businesses which intrigues because of the many variables. You have to try and guess which items will prove to be best sellers. You have to try to gauge the prospective market with some accuracy, and you have to be a little bit of a psychologist to determine what it will take to persuade people to buy from you. Sometimes you need just a little spark of inspiration.

HOW TO OBTAIN MONEYMAKING INSPIRATION

The greatest inspiration of all is watching your ideas and efforts come to fruition. Success breeds success. But with every venture there are times when your confidence needs a little boost. There are times when your mind seems to be bogged down in a bottomless quagmire and you badly need that flash of inspiration.

Don't wait for it to come, make it come. Give yourself a mental shot in the arm and discover the tremendous exhilaration of having your mind flooded with new ideas and exciting possibilities. Give your brain a line of new avenues to explore.

By now you are beginning to realize the tremendous value of the information provided by newspapers, magazines, trade books and telephone directories. Make a special effort to read through these gold mines regularly.

Just reading through, watching for information about new businesses and studying the advertisements will continue to provide a constant stream of ideas. But for the really big idea, you need the magic of inspiration. You need that great flash of mental lightning that sparks the real moneymaking ventures. It will never come of its own accord. You have to take positive steps to galvanize your mind into profitable activity. Here's how you can take those very rewarding steps.

Sit down in a comfortable armchair with your daily selection of newspapers, making notes of those items which interest you. When you have gleaned as much useful information as possible, put the papers to one side and let your mind digest what you have just read. Make no attempt to direct your thoughts, just let your mind dwell on whatever possibilities it wishes to consider, even if at this time they may seem only remotely concerned with the business of making money.

Two things will happen. First, you'll start a train of thought where one idea leads to another. One of those ideas could be the very inspiration you seek. Second, those thoughts which are running through your mind have a strange way of sorting themselves out without any conscious effort and then popping back into your mind as a clear cut proposition at a later date—sometimes when you least expect it.

Never ignore such ideas. These are the ones which seem to be flashes of inspiration because we tend to forget that we have already fed our mental computer with most of the necessary information. Sometimes, when that information is incomplete, the mind is unable to formulate a comprehensive plan. Then, some time later, subsequent data goes into the mind which adds together all the necessary facts and presents you with the answer. It could be that you are completely unaware of all this activity going on somewhere in your mind.

Dianne R. started her train of thought going when she bought a new camera. The salesman opened the box, removed the camera and case, the warranty card and the instruction book. He also took from the box a small canvas bag which he threw into the trash can.

"What was that?" Dianne asked. "That's silica gel," the salesman explained. "They put a small bag of crystals in with each camera to protect it from dampness during shipping. It absorbs moisture from the air, but if we leave it in the box and forget to explain about it, people think that it should be added somewhere to the camera; so we just remove it."

Dianne turned her attention to the new camera and the salesman's instructions for using it. All thoughts of silica gel were dismissed from her mind. Or were they?

Several months later, Dianne tentatively considered starting a small mail order business in order to provide herself with a little extra cash to support her photographic hobby. She had read about the money to be made in mail order, but deciding what to offer became a problem.

It was an article in the daily paper that started her mind racing. She read about a woman who preserved flowers by drying them in a box containing silica gel, and remembered that the camera store was probably still throwing away dozens of these packets every week.

The rest hardly needs telling. Dianne R. collected several silica gel packets from the camera store, tried the flower drying for herself and found it successful. Today, her mail order package of drying box, dessicant chemical and instruction book are bringing her $2,000 a month from a steady stream of orders sent by people who read an advertisement which begins, "You can now preserve your favorite blooms."

Dianne had let her mind travel along paths unfamiliar to her and it rewarded her with more money than she had ever considered possible. Her mail order advertisement was attractive and she reached the right customers. She was also helped with some very useful free publicity. This type of publicity can be yours if you want it.

HOW TO GET FREE PUBLICITY

Almost every magazine has a section devoted to new · products. Sometimes it is the policy of the magazine to examine and critically review the new products they mention. Other magazines simply reproduce photographs of the product and give a few paragraphs of description and explanation.If you would like the magazine you have selected for your advertising to mention your product, write to them, giving a full description of your product, its uses and advantages to the consumer and, where economically possible, offer to send a sample for the magazine to review. Quite often the magazine will be satisfied to receive a clear photograph and a few paragraphs of description.

The magazines which will review and release information on your product do not necessarily have to be those in which you intend to advertise. Many magazines are on the lookout for news of new products in order to keep their readers fully informed of the latest developments in the field in which they specialize.

Another opportunity for you to receive some very valuable publicity in exchange for the cost of your product is by taking advantage of television giveaway shows.

A letter to the program director of those shows which you think may be interested in giving away your product as a prize to winning contestants will often enable you to reap big dividends. Simply state that you would like to offer your merchandise in exchange for a brief commercial during the show.

A similar approach may be taken with regard to the competitions offered by shopping centers. The public relations directors of the larger shopping centers are always seeking ways of promoting business, and quite frequently they stage competitions in which general merchandise is given away as prizes.

If this type of publicity is suitable for your type of merchandise, simply write to the public relations directors of some of the better known shopping centers, offering your product as a prize in their next promotion. The merchandise is offered to the center free, for use as they wish in return for publicity in all their promotional releases.

This tie-in of your product with someone else's promotion can often be very advantageous. Rex W. breeds tropical fish in his spare time. He specializes in guppies, mollies and angels. His sales are mostly to retail stores and occasionally at swap meets.

It was while he was at a swap meet that a man asked him if he would be interested in providing a number of angelfish for a promotion in a large jewelry store. When the proposition was explained in more detail, Rex said that he would be very interested in participating.

Two months later, the jewelry store ran a big promotional campaign and one of the most interesting attractions was a super-sized fish bowl filled with 165 angelfish. In the center of the bowl were suspended two very expensive wrist watches; a man's and a lady's. Customers were invited to guess how many fish there were in the tank in order to win the watches. In all the publicity put out by the jewellers, a mention was made that the fish were supplied by courtesy of XYZ Pet Store, who were major buyers of the fish bred by Rex. The results of the promotion proved to be very satisfying to all concerned.

Promotions such as these surround you at all times. Devise ways in which you can offer your product as a promotional item. All of your efforts to promote the merchandise you have to sell, require that you organize your time to give you the opportunity to accomplish all the things you have to do. Streamlining is one of the ways in which you can use every minute of your spare time to its fullest advantage.

STREAMLINING FOR EFFICIENCY

Your spare time is the time you have at your disposal after you have completed all of your obligatory duties. Since it is spare time it is limited in quantity, so you have to make every minute of it count.

Start by watching your spare-time activity in a way which is completely objective. Pretend you are one of the companies which tell big business how to use time efficiently. These companies watch how the employees of a business carry out their duties. The results of their observations are analyzed, and then suggestions are put forward to tell employers how to achieve the same results in less time and with less wasted effort.

These experts watch for needlessly duplicated movement. They watch for unnecessary procedures and they watch for activities which consume time in a way which could be avoided by alternative methods.

In every business, whether it's a nine-to-five regular job or a spare time venture which you conduct from seven until eleven in the evening, it is only natural to fall into a comfortable routine. This can be a very effective way of ensuring that all the things which have to be done are carried out in a way which is almost automatic. It helps you to avoid inadvertently missing an essential step. For instance, can you imagine mailing 50 letters and forgetting to put postage stamps on them? If you have an established routine, such mistakes may be avoided.

But routines also present their own hazards, and it is in carefully examining your own routines that you can make sure that your precious minutes are not slipping by wastefully.

Barry B. converted his large basement into a mail order warehouse. On his way home from work every evening, he would stop off at the post office and pick up his mail. As soon as he had finished his evening meal, he would retire to the basement, open the mail and begin work on his spare-time business.

The orders were entered into an invoice book, letters were set aside to be answered, and the checks and money orders were verified before being placed in a small box.

Barry B. then typed out the necessary self-adhesive labels and took them and the invoices over to a bench where he packed and wrapped his products. The packing boxes were stacked under the bench according to size; wrapping and adhesive tape were ready at hand in dispensers. The walls of the basement were racked with shelves on which his products, a variety of kitchen gadgets, were laid out in neat rows.

Barry B. had a routine and it was working for him. As business increased and his line of products expanded, he built more shelves and worked slightly longer hours. But there came a time when he found he was working to capacity. Orders continued to grow in number, but now Barry was having to leave some over for the following evening which began to upset the routine for the following day. He was trying to go faster and faster, but found that he was actually beginning to go slower and slower. It was time to revise his system.

The answer came almost as soon as he realized what was happening. A check through his files quickly confirmed that there were items which were ordered far more frequently than others. A reorganization of his shelves brought all the more popular items together, close to the packing bench. Instead of several trips to different parts of the room, he could now almost reach out from the packing bench to get the items he needed.

You too, can streamline for efficiency. Buy an appointments book and use it to plan your day-to-day activities. Develop a routine which is comfortable for you and then before it becomes established, check and recheck to see if slight changes in the routine could improve its efficiency.

There is one more area where improved efficiency can pay big dividends, and this is in the way you keep a check on customers, their orders and the cash they send.

RECORD SYSTEMS THAT BUILD PROFIT

To build an efficient, moneymaking mail order business, you need a system which will give you a record of every transaction. You need to know quickly and accurately, who ordered what and when. You need to know the value of the order, whether it was paid cash in advance, and when and where it was shipped.

The system that you devise must be flexible and easy to change as your business changes in character. Above all, however, your system must be simple.

Try to imagine how it would be if you had a period of illness and someone else had to take over at a moment's notice. Could they take a glance at your record stystem and know exactly how you were running your business? If not, your present system is too complicated.

Further along in the book we will be dealing with bookkeeping as it applies to profit and loss ledgers, taxes and general accounting. But what you require in this instance are methods of stock control and customer reference which will allow you a maximum of information, and will readily tie in to your annual or semi-annual bookkeeping. By planning ahead you can save yourself considerable work. Nothing is more frustrating than checking back through several months of records in search of information necessary to complete state or federal tax returns.

At the outset you will need six sets of records:

1. Orders Received
2. Sales
3. Purchases
4. Expenses
5. Customer Index
6. Advertising Analysis

It really doesn't matter whether you use books, looseleaf binders or a card filing system, providing you maintain them religiously. Using a book does eliminate the possibility of loose pages or filing cards becoming mislaid or incorrectly filed, but there is some loss of flexibility. Whichever system you decide to use, the most important part is how thoroughly you take care of it.

The orders received page should be ruled into sections headed: Customer's Name, Address, Order and Unit Price, Cash Received, Date Order Dispatched.

The sales book is simply a running commentary on your sales and can be part of your inventory control. It makes little difference if you have only two or three products or several dozen. It will tell you which items are selling well and which are returning the greatest profit.

Again, divide the sheet by ruled lines. Use a separate sheet for each product, arrange them alphabetically and head each column with: Date, Quantity in Stock, Quantity Sold, Item Value and Total Sales Value.

At the end of each month, run a total and draw a line under each column. This will give you immediate information on which items are selling and the total sales value of that item per month. By having a column for the Item Value, you can show any increase or decrease in price.

Purchases are again best recorded by providing a separate page for each product. You will need columns headed: Date, Quantity Ordered, Wholesale Price (each), Selling Price (each), Quantity Received, Date, Invoice Total.

Expenses is a listing of all the expenses you incur on a day-to-day basis. You will need columns for telephone, electricity, printing and all the other expenses which become part of the business. You can include advertising in this book, but it will be to your advantage to keep a separate analysis of the results of your advertising. The expense totals should be tallied at the end of each month and a line ruled under each column.

Your advertising book should have a copy of your advertisement pasted in the center of one page at the beginning of a section devoted to providing information as to the results of that advertisement. You will need information on the date the advertisement appeared, the medium in which it appeared, the number of responses to the advertisement, the date of those responses and any observations to be made on anything connected with the publication of the advertisement, such as a special anniversary issue of the magazine or a review of your product which directed attention to the advertisement.

ADVERTISING TECHNIQUES

If your advertisement is going to appear in more than one publication, you are going to need key information to tell you which advertisement is being answered. The usual way of obtaining this information is by putting a key word in the address to which customers will reply. A typical key word, for instance, is Dept. A-7; with the letter indicating the magazine and the number indicating the month in which the advertisement appeared. If you prefer, your key word could indicate the magazine by using the first letter of its title. For example, PM-5 could be **Popular Mechanics**, May issue or LC-2 could be **Ladies Circle**, February issue.

Keep your advertising analysis current and it will provide a brightly lit highway for you to follow on your route to your first million. It doesn't matter how small you are when you start, it's how big you are when you finish that really counts.

HOW TO TURN LIMITED CAPITAL INTO UNLIMITED SUCCESS

Cutting corners is no novelty to anyone getting started in business. It is always necessary to spend some money and it becomes a matter of priorities. J. Paul Getty once gave advice to a young man getting started. "Don't spend your money until you've got it to spend," he said.

Many people get started in their own business, spare-time as well as full-time, and they do so with dreams of unlimited wealth: a big house, expensive cars, a boat and a life of ease and luxury.

Sure, all those things can be yours—will be yours if you know exactly what you want and need them badly enough. But as Mr. Getty was trying to say, you can't live in the house until it is built.

It's good to dream, it is even essential. Dreaming gives you a target at which to aim and it helps you to continue persevering when the going seems all uphill. But as Kipling put it, "If you can dream nor let dreams be your master, . . ."

Cut corners by sticking stamps on by hand instead of renting an expensive postage machine. Certainly the machine would save time and time is money, but how much time would it save? At the beginning, which do you have most of—time or money?

Cut corners by using old lumber to make shelves. Buy used office equipment instead of purchasing the latest and most expensive. Go to the corner drug store and pay 10¢ to make a copy of a document you need copied instead of renting or buying an elaborate copying machine.

Of course, new office equipment, chairs, desks and thick carpeting look good. They give you prestige and they make you feel as if you are an immediate business tycoon. But you are buying the appearance instead of earning it and the money you are spending could purchase the products which might really help you to get into the high income brackets. So take it easy at first.

If you are going to manufacture your own products, you can cut corners when you are getting started by making prototypes which will photograph like the real thing and will enable you to provide an illustration with which to test your potential markets without becoming involved in full-scale production.

Rex S. wanted to offer a series of small booklets which would tell people how to dry fruit, how to train dogs, how to care for lawns and how to take care of swimming pools. He knew he could write the booklets because they were based on previous job experiences and he had already written several articles for various magazines which dealt with these subjects. At a later date he would expand the series of booklets into a small library.

He spoke to the printer about the production of the booklets and between them they decided that a 28-page booklet, with soft covers and measuring about five by seven inches would be an ideal way to get started. The booklets would cost about 15¢ each and sell for about $2. The snag was that in order to arrive at a low unit price, the booklets would have to be printed in lots of 5,000 which would present Rex with an initial printing cost of $320 per title and $1,280 for the series of four booklets.

Rex S. was sufficiently confident that the booklets would sell. Consequently, he was quite prepared to invest that amount of money plus the cost of advertising. Caution, however, persuaded him that he should test the market first. He wrote the copy and prepared the illustrations ready for an influx of orders.

He then prepared four covers using the type of card that would eventually be used for the finished product, and made up dummy booklets using plain paper inserts between the covers. The printing on the covers was simulated by using Letraset ® rub-off lettering which costs only a few cents per cover. Rex then had the four dummy booklets photographed and made up an advertisement which he placed in a Sunday newspaper shopping supplement.

The response was immediate. Checks and money orders began pouring in and Rex knew that he was on his way. Today he has more than 50 titles—not all of the booklets were written by himself, but all are published under his mail order name. He still keeps the booklets to a $2 price tag, but increased volume has brought his printing costs down to 12¢ per booklet and he is contemplating buying his own printing press. It might be worth it to him at this time because he has now reached sales of more then 500 booklets a week and he says he hasn't even gotten started yet.

Part of Rex's success is because he is now combining mail order with direct mail. Although his advertisements still mention only four or five booklets, his orders are dispatched together with a thank-you note and a catalogue listing all of the titles. Working from his mailing lists, he sends a monthly catalogue to all his customers and it is quickly paying for his new house in the suburbs.

In your steps toward becoming a master of mail order, it is necessary for you to learn every aspect of the business. Closely tied to mail order is its big brother, direct mail.

Chapter 5

How to Make Direct Mail Pay Off

Direct mail is the most widely used form of advertising in the world. More money is spent on advertising by direct mail than on any other form of advertising.

Direct mail is completely flexible. It can be sent to a few people or to a million. It can be used by a one-man business or a million dollar company. It can follow any style or format within the rules and regulations of the post office and the dictates of decency.

Direct mail produces an extraordinary response, even from those who claim they ignore this type of advertising. Yet this dynamic form of advertising is never covered by most schools of advertising; it is disregarded by many established advertising agencies and is disliked intensely by other media.

But all the tremendous power of persuasion which can be applied by direct mail is yours if you know how to use it.

EXCLUSIVE PRODUCTS AND HIGH PROFITS

Direct mail can give the one-person spare-time business the same sales potential as the well-staffed super store in a major city. Just like the Colt .45 in the Old West, direct mail makes all men the same size.

But there are ways in which you can give your direct mail venture more power than that achieved by many of your competitors. The most effective of these is the exclusive product. The product which only you can offer to the public will build your direct mail muscle faster than any other approaches to the business.

Exclusive products can rocket you to a fortune, but first you must know where you can acquire a product for your own exclusive use, how to safeguard your ability to sell that product, and the best methods of marketing it.

Begin your search for exclusive products by perusing the advertisements for distributors in trade magazines. Apply to manufacturers in your own locality and ask about new products. Advertise for products in your local newspaper and in the major newspapers of the larger cities. Watch for news of new inventions or new approaches to familiar products.

When you have made contact with a supplier of a new product, it is your task to convince them that you can market that product. You must also be able to handle the advertising and be responsible for distribution and the filling of all orders.

Major companies will of course have their own, well-established chain of distribution, coupled with extensive advertising facilities. Smaller manufacturers, however, will often be interested in having someone handling the selling of their product, providing they believe that person to be competent.

The biggest snag in handling an exclusive product, is the problem of ensuring continuing supplies. It can be extremely discouraging to produce a successful direct mail brochure, receive an avalanche of orders and then be unable to supply due to difficulty in obtaining the product.

If you manufacture the product yourself or supply a specialized service, the problem of shortage of supplies will not apply; although in manufacturing your own product it would be necessary to make sure that components and material are not going to dry up on you.

Marketing the exclusive product is much easier than marketing a product with which the public is familiar, providing:

1. That the product fills a consumer need.
2. That the product is not overpriced.
3. That the direct mail literature is attractive and compelling.

Coupled with the attractive brochure and the exclusive product is one other factor which must be taken into consideration. This is that your direct mail advertising must go to the people most likely to buy that product. You would anticipate small success in trying to sell farm tractors to the residents of tenement buildings in New York. It follows that your mailing list must be up-to-date, accurate and divided into classifications to suit your business.

METHODS OF BUILDING A MAILING LIST

Mailing lists may be bought. There are firms which specialize in the preparation and sale of mailing lists. Their fees range from about $40 per 1,000 names for easily produced classifications such as pilots, home owners, swimming pool owners and boat owners. These names and addresses are readily obtainable from registration authorities, swimming pool manufacturers and magazine subscription departments.

More difficult to accumulate are lists comprising such classifications as: people who wear size ten shoes, blonde children and gold prospectors. Such lists may be available, but they would be much more expensive. Yet if you are interested in mailing to any of these classifications, or in fact any clearly defined group of people, you can compile your own listings with just a small amount of effort.

To compile your own mailing list, start by writing to the circulation department of magazines likely to be read by the groups of people in which you are interested. Regardless of how specialized those groups may be, there is almost certainly a magazine aimed directly at those people.

For example, **Canadian Fisherman** and **Ocean Science** is read by people interested in new developments in oceanography. **American Dry Cleaner** is read by professional dry cleaners and shoe repair shop owners read **Master Shoe Rebuilder** magazine.

Most magazines will sell copies of their subscription lists at a reasonable rate and these lists are always up-to-date. If readers change address, they usually inform the magazine to which they have subscribed in order to continue receiving the magazine.

Telephone directories will provide you with mailing lists of businesses and associations, while the voter's registration lists will give you the names and addresses of specific residential areas. This type of listing is useful when you want to blanket a certain area or housing tract with a mailing.

Probably of most importance to you are the listings that you build for yourself from your file of satisfied customers. The people on those lists may have been a customer for one type of product, but they were satisfied with their purchase and they know you are a business to be trusted. Consequently, if you offer them another product, even if it is far removed from the previous purchase, you will be surprised at their enthusiastic response.

That type of list can only be compiled from a list of people whom you have already contacted. When you are starting completely from scratch, there are a few more ways of reaching the very people who are interested in your specific product. The most effective lists come from combining direct mail with mail order. This is achieved by placing an advertisement in a magazine describing the product you have to sell and inviting people who are interested to send for a free brochure.

PROFESSIONAL CALCULATIONS AND AMATEUR GUESSWORK

Magazine advertising is very inexpensive **providing** your profits far exceed the cost of your advertisement. That would seem to be the most obvious statement you have ever read, yet there are countless people who venture into direct mail and mail order and place advertisements in magazines without any apparent forethought at all.

All advertising must have a purpose. You could place an advertisement which persuades people to send money for a product, to visit a certain location or to feel that they would get better results from Product A than they do with the more familiar Product B. But beneath this specifically directed advertising can be a more subtle theme, and it is this hidden motivation which interests us at the moment.

John C. had devised an ingenious electronic climate control for small greenhouses. He first attempted contacting the manufacturers of small greenhouses and tried to interest them in his product. They conceded that it was an effective and desirable way of controlling humidity, but to include it in their present manufacturing program would increase the costs of their product considerably, as the humidity controller was not an inexpensive item. This increase in costs could make them a victim of the closely matched competition in the domestic greenhouse field.

John decided that he would have to go directly to the owners of greenhouses, especially those with the smaller, backyard type of enclosure. He contemplated purchasing direct mail lists from the manufacturers of the greenhouses, but these proved to be more numerous than he had imagined and the number of lists would have proved to be too expensive. So he decided to advertise in one of the gardening magazines and it was then that he had the inspiration which was to set him firmly on the road to success.

John wisely decided against advertising his humidity controller in the magazine. The price would have proved an obstacle to sales unless a persuasive description of the product could be included in the advertisement. The humidity controller had so many ingenious and exciting features that the space needed for a full description would have made the advertisement very costly.

He could have simply given a general description of the product and invited people to send for a brochure, but he considered that unless he could give a fairly full description, people wouldn't even be bothered to send for the brochure. So he decided to offer a premium.

Using his knowledge of climate control, John wrote a small booklet called "What You Should Know About Greenhouse Humidity," and then had 2,000 printed at a cost of $300. He then arranged for a major seed packaging firm to supply him with a special selection of seeds specially suited to greenhouse production. These cost him 10¢ per packet in quantities as required.

The advertisement that John G. placed in the magazine offered his booklet for $1, and with every order he would send three packets of the specially selected seeds free. The customers who sent for the booklet also received an exciting, double page, two-color folder which described the humidity controller in full detail. The folder showed comparative pictures of plants and fruit grown under normal greenhouse conditions and pictures of similar plants grown under humidity control conditions.

Eight months after his first advertisement appeared, John C. sold his entire humidity control business including customer lists, stock and all manufacturing rights to one of his customers for $400,000. He is presently developing an electronic soil sterilization device which he intends to market in the same way.

The entire success of John C.'s venture is based on his ability to accurately judge the possible amounts of profit after all expenses have been taken into consideration, between two different methods of applying direct mail techniques.

There are customers waiting to buy from you. Every product and every service can be sold at a profit. It all rests on your ability to put yourself in the place of the customer and decide which approach would be the most effective.

THAT INEXHAUSTIBLE MOUNTAIN OF GOLD

Take a look at the street on which you live and then think about all the houses and all the men and women and children who live in those houses.

Now start thinking about neighboring streets, gradually letting your mind go free to visualize all the people in your town, then finally, the state. There are thousands and thousands of them, and so far you are only contemplating the one state! When you really get down to thinking about it in those terms, you gradually begin to realize, perhaps for the first time, just how many people there are in the entire country. Each one of them, figuratively speaking, spends money every day of every week of every month of every year—even if it's only on food.

So now let's imagine that the product you have to offer is a bathroom accessory. Can you imagine just how many bathrooms there are? Or let us imagine that you are marketing

an item for young children. You have before you a market which
is almost impossible to saturate; **and every person in the
country can be reached by mail.**

If you intend to take those moneymaking steps to your first
million, the time to do it is **now.** Not next week or next month,
not even tomorrow—**now.**

That doesn't mean that you have to dash about making off-
the-cuff decisions, but it does mean that from now and until the
bank manager beams whenever you enter the bank, you have to
start pointing all your spare time at a specific target.

HOW TO GET STARTED

Begin by sitting quietly and considering all the aspects of
mail order and direct mail that you have just read. Now glance
around the room in which you are sitting and you will realize
that every single object in that room could have been bought
through the mail.

Does that come as a surprise? If it does, you are in for
another one. That same fact applies to the entire house. There is
hardly anything at all in your house that could not have been
bought by mail order or direct mail. And if you really get down
to it, even the plumbing, the electrical work, the plastering and
the construction of the house itself could have been learned by
means of a mail order course of instruction.

Now, all you have to do is to decide what you think you can
sell at a competitive price in a challenging market. Facing you
at the other end of a postage stamp is a great, inexhaustible
mountain of gold. You have the knowledge you need to be able to
buy at low prices, you know how to get best value for your advertising dollar and you know how to explore your markets.

The gold is waiting to be mined, but there are still one or two
areas of mail order of which you should be aware. Areas which
can help make your success even more certain.

HOW TO ELIMINATE THE NUMBER ONE PROFIT KILLER

As with every business, time wasted is the biggest enemy. In a spare-time business, wasted time can kill profits faster than any other form of business inefficiency. In an extreme case it can even reduce a successful business to complete failure.

Time can be wasted in several ways and it will be worth your while to examine them and take steps to ensure that your business is not even slowed by errors in time management.

One of the problems is that time mangement errors are often difficult to spot unless you know for what it is you are watching. A problem in one area can throw an extra burden on another area, eventually causing an entire venture to become sluggish and inefficient.

For example, Jim W. sold a fishing lure which he had designed and was having manufactured locally. His direct mail brochure, sent to addresses from lists supplied by sports magazines, was a real winner and his business quickly grew to a point where every spare minute of his time was occupied.

Jim W. operated through a post office box located in a neighboring city. His local post office, old and unable to meet the demands placed on it by a rapidly growing community, had no boxes available and there was a long waiting list for boxes which were relinquished.

For two years, Jim's business continued to grow and he worked every available minute until he reached the point of contemplating leaving his regular employment and working on his spare-time venture full time. It was then that he suddenly realized that the old post office had been replaced by a modern, much larger building with enough boxes to meet the demands of the area.

Although Jim had noticed the building being erected, he had become so accustomed to taking his 20 minute drive to the neighboring city and 20 minute drive back every day, the thought of getting a new box had never occurred to him.

When the needless loss of time was brought to his attention by a friend, Jim W. immediately applied for and obtained a local box. He changed the address on his mailing pieces and found that he then had sufficient time saved every week to build his business for another year. At that time, his decision to go into the direct mail business full time made success more certain.

Wasted time may be discovered in routine procedures where actions are needlessly duplicated. It may occur when products prove to have faults and time is lost replacing the item and in writing letters of apology.

A direct mail business is competitive. Even when you have an advantage with an exclusive product, that advantage will only be temporary. Eventually, your competitors will be making every effort to catch up, while you, of course, are making every effort to stay out in front.

Watching your time management will always be to your advantage, but there are a few other moneymaking steps you can take to compete with the really large mail order firms.

HOW TO COMPETE WITH THE GIANTS AND WIN

The really big mail order companies have a big advantage over you, the small spare-time business, and they use that advantage to the hilt. They have a great deal of money.

The major companies can afford to have beautiful color-filled catalogues printed and, if they wished, they could mail one to every home in the United States. They can afford to employ top flight artists, market research teams and financial wizards to tell them how to stay financially sound.

In having all these very real advantages, however, they must lose out on others; some of which can be equally as important as those already mentioned.

First, perhaps more important than anything else, they sacrifice the personal touch—the ability to give individual attention to every detail of the operation. In your business, you and you alone are responsible for its operation. You may, of course, have someone helping you address envelopes or package goods, but it remains your responsibility.

Second, and this also comes within the province of the previous advantage, your customers receive personal attention. Providing personal attention to customers is just about the fastest way to build any business.

Third, your budget will be small compared with the big companies. This, too, can be an advantage. You will be less likely to take risks on doubtful products, you will take every step to save yourself unnecessary expenditure, and when you do launch a product which doesn't do as well as you had hoped (and this happens eventually to everyone in business), your losses will be small compared with that suffered by the larger companies.

There is one other way in which you can compete favorably with the big mail order companies and that is by using the same principles that are used in ju-jitsu and karate. You use the strength of your opponent against himself.

Here's an example, not in the field of mail order. Herbie R. successfully used this method of business building on his way to a fortune.

It had taken Herbie a long time to save enough money to open a store in a rapidly expanding part of town. He intended to sell bicycles and accessories. It is easy to imagine his dismay when two weeks after opening his store, one of the major bicycle and accessory chain stores opened a branch just two doors away. He was faced with competing against a company with unlimited resources and one which indulged in tremendous newspaper and television advertising.

Herbie proved more than equal to the situation. He began by making an effort to stock items not stocked by the bigger company. He emphasized the personal approach and, with a touch of genius, he changed his own advertising slightly to read, "Herbie R.—Only a few steps away from XYZ."

Within two years the big company made an unbelievable offer to Herbie offering to buy him out. He told them that if they would like to double their offer he would sell. They eventually agreed, but on the condition that he didn't re-open again in competition, and Herbie was happy to agree.

Herbie R. was an individualist. His own special brand of salesmanship was stamped on everything he did. The distinctive approach will win business in every field. In direct mail it is particularly effective. Make **individualism** one of your longest steps toward your first million.

YOUR OWN INDIVIDUAL SPARE-TIME MONEYMAKER

The value of exclusive products was mentioned in an earlier chapter. Direct mail can be such a person-to-person business that a first-class, exclusive product can be offered for sale for quite a long time before a competitor gets wind of it.

How to discover, manufacture and merchandise your own exclusive product has also been covered previously, but there are one or two personal assets you probably have never considered as direct mail items. Here are just three to consider and you can probably think of many more.

1. Send a letter to small businesses, offering to write their advertising copy for them. The letter should be short, to the point and, if possible, include several samples of your work. If you have no samples of actual work to show, write a few examples of the type of work you can do. Your fees for such work should be based on the time taken to do the work your clients require, and $10 an hour would be a reasonable rate to charge.

2. Offer to teach by mail on a person-to-person basis, a subject on which you are knowledgeable—how to take photographic

portraits; how to avoid probate; how to grow orchids or how to repair domestic appliances.

Any of these subjects and many, many more offer your customers an opportunity to start their own spare-time business and you could mention this in your advertising. The fees you ask for such tuition could range from $150 to $600.

3. Genealogical Research. There are a great number of people who are interested in knowing their lineage. If you have an interest in detective work of this type, genealogical research could be an excellent direct mail subject.

The fees you would be able to charge for this type of work can vary considerably. Fees plus "expenses" can amount to several thousand dollars for a full search. People who specialize in genealogical research, reach for the more wealthy clientele, and the quest for information could bring you into contact with people in many different countries.

Genealogical research is not only an absorbing pursuit but it is also ideally suited to spare-time work and can prove extremely lucrative. There are many books devoted to the subject of genealogy. If this type of work suits you, the public libraries can provide a mine of information on how to carry out this type of investigation.

Direct mail has so many possibilites that it is almost impossible to exhaust them. Even the side-shoots can bring you a substantial supplementary income.

HOW TO CASH IN ON DIRECT MAIL SPINOFFS

Any business in which you become involved should always be studied to make sure that every penny of profit is gathered from the venture. There are often areas which, if carefully scrutinzed, will reveal moneymaking possibilities. In direct mail, one of the more obvious opportunities to earn extra money is in the sale of copies of your mailing lists. Most firms which specialize in selling these lists have varying charges for different types of lists. Lists which are fairly easy to compile, such as house owners, company presidents and magazine subscribers, are rated at about $40 per 1,000.

Lists which are more difficult to compile (sometimes to the extent that you have had to accumulate the names carefully over a period of many months) are of course priced at a higher rate. Such lists could, for instance, consist of people who have done dressmaking, are vegetarians or sing in church choirs. The more specialized the list, the higher fees it will command.

When you are firmly established in the direct mail business, you will gradually acquire business machines which save a considerable amount of time. One of the most important of these is the addressing machine.

There are several different types on the market, but basically they all do the same thing. They provide a plate or card for each customer and these cards are fed into the machine, together with a batch of unaddressed envelopes. Then, at a touch of a button or a crank of a handle, the letters are addressed and ejected from the machine at an extremely fast rate.

This system of envelope addressing not only saves time, but it permits systematic filing and cross-indexing by area, employment, financial status or whatever classification you require.

There is one more advantage. With this type of machine, you can offer an addressing service to other firms and businesses. The usual charge for this service is 3¢ per letter.

Who would require such a service? Any businessman who wants to mail advertising to his customers or to prospective customers on lists you have for sale.

In addition to the addressing machine, there are other machines particularly suited to the direct mail business which can also be used to offer a service.

Brochure folding machines, postage machines, packaging machines and saddle stitch machines are always good for extra profit when put to work for other people in addition to the use you make of them.

Finally, there is one further opportunity of making money from a spinoff of your direct mail business—one which is often overlooked, but as it is a vital part of direct mail, it is well worth considering.

Before you engage in either mail order or direct mail, you will have undertaken a reasonable amount of research to ensure that the money you invest in magazine advertising, printing and mailing is money used as effectively as possible.

You will have checked the circulation of the magazines, the type of readership with regard to location, financial status, age and sex. You have examined mailing lists to make certain that all the names and addresses fall within the area you wish to cover.

In some instances, you may have conducted test runs or followed a mailing with a door-to-door canvas to ensure as fully as possible that what you were mailing was read, understood and remembered.

All of this research took both time and money. The information you collected is very valuable to the extent that many people in all types of businesses, including other mail order firms, would be interested in buying that hard-earned information.

The amount you could charge would entirely depend on the extent of your research and its value to the prospective purchaser. But information of this type is never inexpensive.

When you enter the wonderful world of spare-time moneymaking, you must take every step which leads you to the top. Examine your business from every angle to make sure that there isn't an area which is, in fact, an unexplored gold mine.

Follow your hunches and follow your own personal lines of interest. In this way you will discover that it is not only your spare time which is bringing home those big money checks, but your recreational interests too, which have started to become very profitable.

Chapter 6

How to Turn Toys into Second Income

It always seems that toys sell no matter how bad the national economy. They have a constant, all-year-round sale with, of course, a great boost at Christmas.

One of the big advantages of entering the toy business is the sheer joy of being young again. Maybe becoming a toy tycoon could be your doorway to a new, enchanting way of life. That old saying about "not having to be crazy but it helps" was probably originated by a toy salesman.

Grownups enjoy playing, too. Fishing and photography top the list of hobbies and pastimes, and philately (stamp collecting) and model railways must tie for third place, with model car racing rapidly gaining popularity.

For the moment, let us consider the money to be made by people with an interest in model railways and all the satellite projects which are part of this engrossing hobby—including the making of bridges, cities, mountains and scenery.

HOW TO BUILD A STEADY INCOME FROM MODEL RAILWAYS

Model railways is another of those hobbies embracing several other hobbies and crafts. While you may not be particularly interested in knowing whether a locomotive is an 0-4-2 or a 4-6-6, you may find modeling miniature mountains in clay or papier maché completely absorbing. Or perhaps the thought of constructing a tiny city filled with miniature houses, stores and maybe a church or two, fills you with delight. Therefore, in model railways there are a great number of projects which could be of interest to you, and everyone of them is a potential money maker.

How to Get Started

There are so many steps towards making money in model railways that it is going to be easier to take them one at a time, pointing out the possibilities of each with suggestions on marketing. It is up to you to tackle the one which interests you the most, building it in your own preferred way of working.

Scenery modeling—trees, shrubs, grass, mountains, streams, lakes, etc. The greatest ambition of all railway modeling enthusiasts is to obtain scenery which is as close to the real thing as possible, but in miniature form.

They are looking for new modeling materials, quicker and easier methods of constructing houses, stations, hotels and stores and they are also interested in purchasing plans of suggested layouts.

The secret of success in this field is to study the books which give information on the modeling of scenery and then let your inventiveness show you how to improve and commercialize these methods.

MARKETING

Your products or "How To" booklets can be distributed through established hobby stores, either by personal contact, through a wholesaler or directly to the public by mail order.

There is money waiting for model railway enthusiasts who have the initiative to go out and seek the business. For example, many of the larger stores would be prepared to rent a well-constructed model railway display. Such displays always attract attention and build sales, especially a month or two before Christmas.

Filmmakers and commercial advertising photographers, especially those making films for television, are often in search of realistic looking model railways. Trains get blown up, bridges collapse and avalanches thunder down on carriages— all with the help of models.

If you have a model railway or even an authentic looking section, write to the major advertising agencies and film companies, offering your facilities for filming.

The fees you charge will depend on the use for which the photographs are intended. As a rule, most film companies have set rates for this type of set rental and the rates are quite generous. So until you have established a reputation as being able to supply models "true to life," be content to leave the question of fee to the advertising agency or film company.

Before leaving the subject of model railways, there are two more moneymaking opportunities which must be mentioned, although you will doubtlessly be able to think of several more.

The first is the taking of photographs which illustrate special methods of model or scenery construction or the use of unusual materials. These photographs would find a ready market with the publishers of model railways magazines.

The second project is a much more ambitious venture, but one which lends itself well to spare-time activities. It is one which has already made a few enterprising people very wealthy.

It is the construction of a large city built completely to scale and covering a considerable area of land. This miniature city would be large enough for people to visit, walking through streets between knee-high houses, passing by lakes with pleasure boats cruising across the water and pausing at remote controlled railway crossings while express trains thunder along a miniature track.

Such a vast project would take considerable time to construct and could be used in any of the previously mentioned ventures while it is being constructed. But once the miniature city is sufficiently completed to attract customers, the money they pay to wander around this Lilliputian world will quickly help in its completion.

Any hobby which has its own devoted enthusiasts is a prime spare-time moneymaking opportunity, and such a hobby is the collecting of dolls. It doesn't take too much imagination to realize that there is considerable money in the doll business. There are thousands and thousands of little girls and they all want dolls. All you need is a plastic injection machine, a few molds, someone to design and manufacture the clothes, several thousand dollars for materials, packaging, advertising and transportation, and you're on your way to a fortune.

That may be the doll business, but it certainly isn't a spare-time venture. Nor is it all of the doll business. Some of the other areas may present difficulties which, while not unsurmountable, would slow down your climb to the top. But there is one area which is open to specialization, and it can bring you a tremendous spare-time income.

DOLLS FOR CONNOISSEURS

These are not the dolls that young children take to bed or pamper with play feeding bottles. These are the special dolls which adults collect and they can provide you with all those special luxuries which so many other people only dream about.

How to Get Started

The market for these very special dolls is extensive and buyers are attracted by advertisements in collectors magazines or by displays in those stores which specialize in dolls.

Selling this type of doll is not difficult. Your biggest challenge is in obtaining the right type of dolls and getting them at a price which will allow you a high margin of profit.

The type of doll which people collect can be ascertained by watching the advertisements of others who deal in this field. The dolls usually fall into one of two groups. One, the antique doll, and two, the national doll.

Antique dolls may be found in many places from garage sales to public auctions—from collectors selling their collection, to dolls found abandoned in dusty attics. An advertisement in the local newspaper stating that you wish to buy old dolls will often bring more results than you might expect. From that point it is only a matter of being selective and firm on the price you wish to offer.

Old dolls may be found in the most unexpected places, so whenever you travel, watch for opportunities to make a good buy. National dolls are a slightly different proposition. Almost every country produces dolls in national dress. From dolls dressed in the uniform of a sentry, complete with bearskin helmet and sword, typical of the guards at England's Buckingham Palace; to those dressed in the uniform of the Swiss Alpine Guards.

Mexico and Spain produce beautifully dressed dolls with many tiered skirts and lace mantillas, while the dolls from Japan are masterpieces of delicacy, often enclosed in glass showcases.

The cheapest way to buy these dolls is directly from the manufacturers, and the quickest, most satisfactory way of

making contact with these manufacturers is by writing to the
trade department of their embassy in this country. You will be
sent names and addresses, catalogues and sales literature.

This type of business will require a certain amount of investment because you will probably be required to purchase a
minumum quantity to make shipping financially worthwhile.
But even this investment may be kept at its lowest level by
concentrating on one country at a time and selecting those
countries where the rate of exchange is favorable—countries
such as Mexico and Japan.

Be content to start slowly, making your contacts with
manufacturers gradually and establishing good credit and trust
between yourself and the manufacturer. Remember, you are
possibly his only representative in this country, so represent
him well.

As you become established, you will find that your
customers are toy wholesalers with whom you are content to
make perhaps ten percent profit. You will also be dealing with
toy shops and the type of stores that sell gifts and novelties. With
these items your profit margin may be about 25 percent. You
will also deal with doll collectors whom you will reach through
magazine advertising and mail order. With these people you
would expect to make between 100 percent and 150 percent
profit—an amount which would adequately cover your advertising costs.

Sometimes you can gain substantially higher percentages
of profit by concentrating all your advertising and selling to one
specific section of the public. This is because there are certain
sections of the public and certain types of merchandise which
allow you a much greater margin of profit.

Take for example, the difference in profit margins between
sugar in your local supermarket with perhaps two or three
percent profit, and the type of gadgets sold by a store which offers equipment and gadgets to professional magicians. Here the
profit margin may well be in excess of 2,000 percent.

Magic tricks have one of the highest profit margins of any type of merchandise. The reason for this is that the customers are paying a great deal of money for the secret behind the trick, while the actual cost of the equipment they are buying is quite low by comparison.

INVENTING, MAKING AND MARKETING MAGIC SPECIALTIES

First, the market. Who buys magic tricks? Amateur and professional magicians of both sexes and ages that range from seven to seventy.

The number of people who are interested in magic is surprisingly large. We are of course talking about the illusion type of magic, not witchcraft. But the market is even more extensive than you would at first suppose, because there are people other than magicians who are always looking for eye-catching illusions or who are interested in contacting people who can create illusions.

This group of people consists of store display manufacturers and those specialists who manufacture the mind bending effects used in movies and on television.

The sword run through the body in a duel on television was a stage illusion in 1850. The store window which shows a faucet apparently suspended in space with a full stream of water running from it is an adaptation of the inexhaustible wine barrel illusion.

The market is there and may be reached by advertising in **Popular Mechanics** or **Magic Magazine**. But how do you get started in this special field?

Getting Started

Nearly all magic is based on three principles: appearance, disappearance and transformation. There are a few illusions

which do not quite fall into these three categories, such as saw-
ing a woman in two or the so called "mental mysteries" using
apparent E.S.P. In becoming involved in magic for money (and
what could be more intriguing?), you'll soon learn to recognize
the type of creativity behind every illusion.

Magic can involve the use of everday objects such as cups
and saucers, playing cards and cigarettes. It can also use living
objects such as doves, rabbits or goldfish; or it can involve specially constructed apparatuses.

There are inventive men whose names have become
associated with certain types of magic: Scarne with cards,
Proudlock with thimbles and Grant with stage illusions. There
are also men whose names are associated with one special
effect such as Chung Ling Soo and his bullet catching mystery.

The secret of inventing magic tricks is to dream of a presentation which could be regarded as completely impossible and
then sit down and plan how you could achieve the impossible.

Let us imagine that you have had the idea of being able to
shuffle a pack of cards and then cut at the ace of spades. The
chances of doing so would be 51 to 1. To do it a second time would
be extremely unlikely. The odds against cutting the ace every
time would be astronomical—unless all the cards were aces.
Too easy? All right, how about doing the same thing with an apparently regular pack. Regular except for the ace of spades
which is slightly wider than all the other cards. Now, when you
go to cut, your fingers can find the ace every time.

There is a great deal of money to be made in the invention
and manufacture of magic tricks. Read every book you can on
the subject and let your own mind visualize spectacular
mysteries. Then, think out your own solution to those
mysteries.

If you can devise a mystery, having it manufactured is no
problem. In some instances you need not even go to the lengths
of manufacturing in order to make money. There are many
tricks sold by stores which have a clientele of professional
magicians, where the customer pays a great deal of money—

sometimes hundreds of dollars—for an original and exclusive idea which would create a reputation for the magician who performs it.

If you can invent magical mysteries, you have no need to be too concerned about marketing them. The demand is such that there will be a waiting list of customers, all wanting something new and exclusive.

Ehrich Weiss worked in a necktie factory during the day. In his spare time he began inventing magical effects. One of his most creative ideas was destined to become famous. It was a trunk which could be locked, padlocked and bound by chains, and from which he could enter or escape at will. Later, Ehrich changed his name to Harry Houdini and began a full-time career in magic. His inventive mind brought him financial success and a world-wide reputation which will never die.

The opportunities for making money are everywhere. From magic tricks to building blocks. From Tinker Toys to radio-controlled model airplanes, opportunities abound. They even face you every morning on the breakfast table.

THE BREAKFAST FOOD FORTUNES

Have you ever wondered about those novelties which are offered in boxes of breakfast cereal? Have you ever wondered who makes them or whether they really do have any effect on sales? Wonder no more. Those tiny plastic novelties have an enormous impact on sales. Children can be really persuasive when they want to be, and the advertising of those novelties is usually extremely compelling.

Who makes them? Usually, the breakfast cereal manufacturer and their advertising agency decide on the giveaway item to be offered and the production of that novelty is contracted with a firm which specializes in that type of item.

Competition in this field is quite fierce and the more interesting or exciting the giveaway novelty, the more keen the cereal producers are to have it.

People who create these small novelties have to work within very strict limitations. The items have to be small, very inexpensive (usually polystyrene), easy to understand and have some functional purpose.

Perhaps it would be a model of a spaceman. A simple product, but the arms and legs will be free to move. It could be an educational product—one of a series of prehistoric monsters with the name of the creature engraved on the base, for example.

How to Get Started

Entering this field requires three different approaches. In the first step, you must be able to visualize a suitable item. Study the shelves of breakfast cereals in your supermarket and you'll soon get an idea of the type of product that is given away in the cereal boxes.

In the second step, you have to be able to make or have made a sample of the product you have visualized. Although the final production may be of plastic, your prototype could be of balsa wood or metal.

For the third step, you must be able to offer your sample to the manufacturer of the food product or his advertising agency. If you can arrange to do this in person, so much the better. However, if you are situated many miles from the people to whom you want to offer your idea, you have no alternative but to mail it. Sometimes it is sufficient to send a description or a drawing of your creation, but a prototype is far more effective.

Payment for ideas of this type can vary considerably, but it is usually on the generous side for two reasons. First, they don't want you to take your ideas to a competitor. Second, they can never by sure that your subsequent ideas are not going to get better and better. If this is so, they want to be sure to have first offer of your new creations.

From breakfast cereal giveaways to model boats is quite a step. But if you get pleasure from making things with your hands, model boats could be exactly what you are looking for.

BIG MONEY FROM MODEL BOATS

Model boats have always possessed a strong fascination for children, and wherever there's a pond or small lake you'll usually find a model boat battling the waves.

Some of the model boats, yachts, schooners and sloops are master-pieces of model ship-building. Members of model sailing clubs get together to hold their own regattas, with prizes for design and for being placed in class races. If your ability as a craftsman is equal to the skills of shipbuilding, there is considerable wealth and pleasure ahead of you.

How to Get Started

Your first step must be to determine in which direction your interests and inclinations are going to lead you; from tiny yachts to spice carrying clippers, or from atomic submarines to radio-controlled galleons. The world of boats and water craft is enormous. Len B. is in his seventies and he has been making models of fishing boats in his spare time since he was 12 years old. He thinks he has sold more than 3,000 of them, mostly to hobby stores. George F. specialized in sloops and clippers of the early 1900's. Although he worked as a post office letter sorter during the day, his spare-time models were so detailed that museums and maritime associations beat a path to his door.

There is always a market for model boats, whether they are sold to young people through retail stores or to the many clubs and associations that display such interests.

Verne A. makes a hefty spare-time income by making tiny desk top replicas of boats. These are finely detailed models of privately owned pleasure boats that are moored in slips at marinas from Long Beach to San Diego. Verne tracks down the owners of the more luxurious crafts and makes an appointment for an interview. He takes along samples of models which have been made into paperweights, pen holders, glass-cased boardroom displays, and living room table lamps. The prices range from $250 to $2,000 which he obtained for a radio-controlled pleasure cruiser destined for a large, privately-owned lake.

Perhaps the most lucrative side of model boats is the construction of galleons for store window displays and the specially constructed galleons with breakaway parts used in film-making. These "special effect" galleons are constructed to take small, electrically detonated charges which blow off the breakaway parts of the ship to simulate direct hits by an enemy vessel.

Although this special market may appear to be limited, there are perhaps only half a dozen people in this field and they are kept busy full time, all year round. So if you think your skill and interest is equal to the task, make a sample model, photograph it and send the photograph together with full information to all of the major film and television studios.

The work you will receive will be on assignment, with the fee based on the specifications of the vessel and the time it would take to produce a finished model.

The rate for this type of model building varies from $15 to $35 an hour depending on your skill, reputation and most important of all, your ability to complete the work by a promised delivery date.

Projects such as this cannot fail to stimulate the imagination. But sometimes it is the imagination, together with a little publicity, that can compensate for lack of manual dexterity. If boat building is beyond your ability, there are other ways to let your imagination guide your steps to that million dollar bank balance.

HOW TO START A CRAZE AND CAPTURE A FORTUNE

If you've never heard of such things as a yo-yo, Biff-Bat Diabalo or hoola-hoop, then you have a big surprise coming. These, and several other similar toys have swept across country after country, building vast fortunes for a great many people.

It is difficult to analyze exactly why certain items build such popularity. Publicity and showmanship help to get the craze started, but if that were all, we would be inundated with new crazes every week. So it must be something more than just publicity.

If you examine the items which have been internationally successful, you will discover they all have certain features in common. They are all simple and inexpensive to manufacture, they are bought and used by both sexes, and they offer a challenge of skill to the user. Is this a field you could enter? Of course. All you need is determination.

There are two steps you can take to start making big money in this field of crazes. The first step is by devising an entirely new item, one which fulfills the above three qualifications, and then introducing it to the public. Of course it is not quite as simple as all that, but as always, the hurdles which have to be overcome eliminate the fainthearted.

The product you devise has not been invented yet so we can't start discussing it. The production and merchandising are fields in which you can become involved if you have the time, money and inclination. But for your first effort, you may find it more convenient to produce a prototype and then sell the idea to a toy manufacturer or to a firm of marketing specialists. This sale may be outright or it could be tied to royalties which are paid to you with every item sold.

Although the money you earn by selling your idea will not be as much as it would be if you were handling the whole thing yourself, this way, financial commitment is minimal. This is a point worth remembering when you are getting started. Later, with more experience and capital backing you, your ventures into this field can be more involved.

The second step is one which gives you more control and in which you can become more involved; although it does sometimes require a small capital investment. This second method requires that you take advantage of existing crazes or revive those that have passed. Certain crazes are perennial. Year after year goes by and at some period during each year, certain items gain great popularity.

Kite flying is a typical perennial craze and so is frog jumping. At one time, spinning and whipping tops were like fevers that gripped young people.

The secret of becoming a toy tycoon—of making money by riding the crest of these pastimes—lies in plotting the seasons during which they are popular and by being prepared to take advantage of them.

The correct way to take advantage of them and become rich in the process is by elevating them and giving them stature. John and Jean L. got caught up in the kite business almost by accident. Their two young sons insisted on having kites flown for them every time they went to the beach.

At first, due to lack of expertise, more kites were ruined than flown. To John, getting a kite to fly high and long became a challenge. He read books about kites and kite flying and was soon designing and flying his own kites.

The hobby eventually became a spare-time business. With his wife Jean, he leased a small store near the beach and filled it with kites of every description, together with all types of kite-building material.

The kite store is open only on Saturdays and Sundays, but for those two days every week, it is filled with kite enthusiasts of every age. The gross takings for those two days will be in excess of $1,500. John had taken a centuries-old hobby—one which at predictable times of the year became a craze—elaborated on it, gave it dignity and began making a great deal of money.

Almost every facet of the toy business will offer you the opportunity to make money in your spare time. You can select the type of toys which interest you personally, and even if your home is small and you feel pressed for space, there are toys which will fit in with the most restricted space.

MINIATURE TOYS AND GREAT PROFITS

The two Lesney brothers had always been interested in automobiles and their venture in making tiny, scale models began almost casually—spare-time interest. Today, their wonderfully detailed series of Matchbox miniature cars may be found in almost every part of the world.

Young and old alike are fascinated by the miniature. Miniature roses, miniature poodles, miniature radios, trees and cameras. The whole world is getting smaller. But doll's houses have enjoyed fantastic popularity for many years. Miniature replicas of popular items will always have a ready market and it's a market that's waiting for you.

How to Get Started

First, let us survey the possiblities. There are three ways in which you can tackle this lucrative field.

1.**Buying and selling.** You simply buy from manufacturers or wholesalers and re-sell. Under this heading you can include the buying and selling of used toys.

2.**Manufacturing.** The making of miniature toys has tremendous possibilities. If you have any manual skill, this is a field well worth considering.

3.**Collector's Items.** This, too, could be considered a combination of the first two possiblities. But it is a very important field, and worth a section all to itself; so we will leave it for now and pick it up again in Chapter 8.

BUYING AND SELLING

The techniques of buying and selling have already been covered, but with miniature toys it will benefit you to concentrate on the unusual—items which are not to be found in every toyshop or drug store.

For example, Brittain of London, England, make a beautiful miniature garden in plastic. All the tiny flowers, shrubs, trees, fences, walls, lawns and fountains are packaged separately and are so designed that they can be planted into a special baseboard to form an endless variety of garden arrangements. The product is unusual and intriguing.

With these tiny gardens in mind, there is a sideshoot venture which may be worth exploring. You may be able to sell professional landscape gardeners complete sets of these toy gardens. Why would they be interested in playing with toys? It's very possible that they could make proof layouts of suggested garden schemes to give prospective customers a visual impression of how their garden would appear when finished. Miniature gardens could be a very good selling tool for the professional landscape gardener.

To find the unusual, subscribe to toy trade magazines, send for manufacturers' catalogues and attend the toy trade shows.

MANUFACTURING

In this field, it is ideal to concentrate on handcrafted items which meet a demand and for which a reasonably good profit may be expected. In this way you can compete favorably with the mass production of plastic toys.

One of the most popular items, and for which there is never sufficient supply, is miniature dollhouse furniture. This must be fully detailed and well-designed. It could even be period pieces, miniature Chippendale chairs or Victorian grandfather clocks.

Concentrate on quality and authenticity and your bank balance will start climbing from your first sale. Miniature or dollhouse scale jewelry, clothing, drapes, table cloths and the like are always in demand.

Even ceramics has unlimited opportunities when applied to the field of dollhouse miniatures. Items such as vases, table lamps, flower pots, cups and saucers, and teapots will always sell well. Pet cats and dogs can also be made in ceramic, as can food on plates ready for serving. Imagine tiny plates loaded with turkey sandwiches, fruit, toast, and cakes.

The dollhouse field is a land of endless opportunity. Your sales may be made through a few carefully selected high class toy stores, or by advertising in magazines offering a free catalogue of your hand crafted products.

Display Models—Under this heading are those window displays which may be seen in many of the larger department stores.

The display could be an old time replica of the store itself constructed with the aid of old photographs. Many stores feature moving displays, especially at Christmas (they begin ordering as early as January). These moving displays are often ready-made toys taken apart and motorized.

This is a specialized field and you would often be working to build models to special requirements. But if tiny dolls that wave, or windmills that turn, or reindeer that fly are a challenge you can't resist, build a sample model and take it or photograph it and send it to the merchandising manager of a few of the leading toy or department stores.

When negotiating a price for your work, base it on an hourly rate of between $10 and $20, for as long as it would take you to construct whatever is called for.

Before leaving the subject of toys, it is worth considering those toys which are of a more instructional nature than simple playthings.

THE MARKET FOR SCIENTIFIC ACCESSORIES

Scientific accessories reach into so many fields—biology, parapsychology, ecology, medicine, photography, astronomy and electronics, to mention just a few. To cover the field thoroughly would take several books this size. So again you must choose the area which interests you the most, and apply your skills to an enterprise which will turn your spare time into a means of becoming wealthy.

Once again, there are opportunities in buying and selling. Government surplus stores, public auctions and classified ads in the scientific apparatus wanted columns of the larger newspapers will provide a source for your purchases. Sales may be made through advertising or to local schools and colleges.

There are many opportunities in manufacturing. Dennis A. makes barographs in the basement of his home. The clock mechanism, the pen, the drum and the barometer are purchased from various manufacturers while the graph paper, polished wood base and mechanical linkage is supplied to him by local industry. The parts cost $18 per completed unit, purchased in lots of 50, while the completed unit sells for $56 through mail order.

Sixteen-year-old Peter V. makes astronomical telescopes in his spare time. He, too, buys the parts from a scientific apparatus supply store. These parts cost him between $150 and $200 per telescope, but his completed instrument sells for $650 to people who write to him on recommendation.

There are so many ways of assembling accessories for use in research or experimentation that the list would be almost endless. But there is another approach to the business of making money with scientific equipment and it is one which is worth considerable attention.

There are many people who make money in their spare time, but because it is a spare-time occupation they are termed amateurs. In many instances, these so-called amateurs make as much money, and sometimes more, than the professional.

Ramon S. lives in a remote farming community and his special interest is meteorology. With his special equipment he provides his community with a continuous weather watch. Even the local radio station includes his forecast in their news bulletins.

Dr. Harry E. Thomason, a patent examiner and attorney for 24 years, has become one of the world's leading authorities on solar heating.

There are many people in all walks of life who spend much of their spare time walking along beaches and parks with a metal detector, and thousands more who are interested in rock and gem polishing and who can earn a very high extra income from custom-made jewelry.

In other words, the field of scientific accessories not only pays off in the sale and manufacturing of equipment, but there is another door leading to unlimited opportunities with the use of such equipment.

From toys to pastimes is a very short step. To some people metal detectors and guns may be considered toys. To the people who use them, however, they can be big business.

Chapter 7

How to Cash In On Popular Pastimes

The United States of America is one of the most pleasure loving countries in the world. Its people take their leisure and recreational activities almost as seriously as they do their work. If you pause for a while and consider the matter carefully, you will probably be quite surprised at the incredible number of recreational activities, and at their wide diversity.

There is surfing, skate-boarding, rock hounding, cycling, electronics, dressmaking, cake decorating, stamp collecting, wood carving, metal sculpture, ceramics and scuba diving—to name just a few. The list is almost endless and every one of them can make you enormously wealthy.

Some of these pastimes, photography and fishing for example, are so popular as to warrant a chapter to themselves. But by taking a few of the slightly less popular ones and examining them, you will soon discover how to apply your own personal touch. You must know how to take your own inclinations and ideas and use them in a way which will bring you vast spare-time dividends.

TREASURE HUNTING MADE PROFITABLE

The modern metal detector continues to gain popularity. As lower priced models and do-it-yourself kits become more readily available, the popularity rating will climb higher and higher.

The most obvious way of making money with a metal detector is by finding hidden treasure. Charles C., searching near the old Butterfield stage line, tracked down a signal from his metal detector and unearthed 202 silver dollars, 79 $20 gold pieces, 53 $10 gold pieces, 43 $5 gold pieces and 2 $2.50 gold pieces. The mint dates covered the period 1850-1881.

It has been said that more money has been buried and lost than has ever been found. So if you'd like to try the real heady wine, take a little spare time, add a dash of adventure combined with fresh air and exercise, sprinkle liberally with luck and who knows? It may be your metal detector that sends out that golden signal.

You can put a few percentage points on your side by doing a little research and concentrating your search on areas which are more likely to provide exciting results. The sites of old settlements, especially near gold and silver mines are high probability areas, as are the routes of old stage coach runs or around old ghost towns.

A great deal more money than you might expect may be made by using a metal detector along beaches or in parks and campgrounds where people gather for picnics. People lose not only money, but rings and other jewelry. Part of the lure of treasure hunting is the fact that you can never be sure what the next beep from your detector will reveal.

Metal detectors can also provide you with a different type of spare-time income. There are now sufficient metal detectors on the market to enable you to advertise the buying and selling of used detectors. For this type of business, you would have to make yourself familiar with the different types of detectors presently available, their technical differences and their prices.

Your business would begin with an advertisement in your local paper—"Used Metal Detectors Wanted for Cash." The price you would expect to pay for a used metal detector would depend very much on its condition, make and performance. But the most you would pay for an instrument in immaculate condition would be just below half the retail price of that model when new.

With one or two models in hand, you would then run a second advertisement offering those models for sale; pricing them to give you a minimum of 50 percent profit, including the cost of any servicing or repairs you may have had to make.

Linked to this type of business could be the repair and servicing of metal detectors for customers. Again, you could attract this type of business with a small advertisement in your local newspaper. If your work is good and your charges reasonable, you could quickly build a substantial metal detector repair service.

As with all spare-time businesses, the metal detector business can be precisely what you make it. Concentrate and put your mind to work.

Ron C. put his mind to work. He lives on the outskirts of a large city and he became aware of the large number of people who were to be seen on weekends combing the beaches and campsites with metal detectors.

He visited a few stores which sold this type of equipment and enquired as to the number of detectors they thought they had sold during the previous 12 months. The answers were sufficient to convince him that the idea simmering in his mind was going to be worth trying.

Ron obtained a dozen brass discs and had them stamped with numbers from 1 to 12. Each disc was about the size of a quarter and in addition to the number, each of them had Ron's initials stamped on the reverse side.

He took the discs to an area of land just outside the city and buried them at varying depths in places scattered over the area, making a careful plan of the location of each disc as he did so. When this was completed, he had a printer run off 100 simple maps showing the area but not the location of the discs.

His next step was to place an advertisement in the three major newspapers of the city. In the advertisement he invited owners of metal detectors to come and search for his brass discs, or "Treasure Keys" as he called them.

Each Treasure Key was worth previously designated amounts which varied from a $5 bill to a diamond and ruby ring. Other prizes included a CB radio, a tape recorder and dinner for two at a well-known restaurant.

The two stipulations which Ron made were that all the participants had to register by letter or telephone the day before the date specified for the hunt. Secondly, before people began searching, they had to purchase one of Ron's maps for $3 which showed them the boundaries of the search area. All Treasure Keys unearthed would only be accepted from people in possession of one of the maps.

The search was set for a Sunday from 9 a.m. to 5 p.m. At 8:30 a.m. Ron set up a tent with props to represent an old time prospector's base camp. He also posted a large sign on which was painted the numbers 1 through 12. As the discs were discovered and brought to him, Ron chalked the finds up on the sign board for the treasure hunters to see. At the same time he gave the finder of each Treasure Key a voucher with which they could collect their prize from a local merchant.

Ron started his moneymaking venture with these thoughts in mind:

1. That not all the discs would be discovered in the eight hour period.

2. If local fishermen would pay $3 to fish in a nearby trout farm, amateur treasure hunters would pay $3 for prizes worth much more.

3. He knew he could arrange with local merchants to supply him with the prizes at a special price.

Ron had expected about 50 participants at the first hunt, but hoped to build that number by holding regular treasure hunting events. In fact, more than 200 eager amateur prospectors came for the first hunt (which was reported on by the newspapers) and 350 for his second. The numbers are still growing and Ron's first prize is now a small car.

At the end of each day's prospecting, Ron discloses the whereabouts of each undiscovered disc and he changes the style of disc and the search area for each event.

Although his profit depends on the number and type of Treasure Keys discovered, and although the bigger prizes are hidden in the more difficult locations, Ron anticipates showing a profit of between $1,000 and $2,000 for each event.

Good ideas will always pay good dividends. Almost every hobby and pastime will offer opportunities for making money. All you have to do is think.

NEW METHODS OF TAXIDERMY

With every spare-time business you contemplate, you will always ask yourself the inevitable question, "What are the chances of success?"

Your answer will be based on the answer to other questions including, "Is there a demand for this?"; "What are the costs, expenses and potential profits?" and "How much competition is there in this particular field?"

With many projects, obtaining answers to these questions will involve a certain amount of research and calculation. In the field of taxidermy, several of the answers you seek are readily obtainable.

1. The demand for stuffed animals, birds, fish and reptiles is considerable. Apart from sports people who like to see their trophies mounted for home decoration, there is a steady demand for well-mounted specimens by museums, colleges, interior decorators and certain businesses.

The businesses which are always in the market for good specimens are retail sports goods stores and the manufacturers of fishing tackle, rifles and ammunition, and archery equipment. Hunting lodges and sporting clubs also purchase well-prepared specimens.

2. The costs and profits must be calculated just prior to getting started. But as you will see in a moment, there is a way in which an investment can cut down on your time and labor costs.

3. Taxidermy is a subject which can be tackled successfully by people of either sex and almost any age. However, it must be something you would like to do.

4. The amount of competition in this field is quite small. A glance at the yellow pages of your telephone directory will quickly confirm this.

It is not the purpose of this section to tell you how to do taxidermy. There are several excellent books which deal with this very thoroughly. But the following information will open your eyes to a most intriguing way to prepare small creatures for exhibition. It is a method which offers possibilities of making you very rich and it is a method which you can pursue casually and in your spare time.

FREEZE-DRYING

While this procedure may not be taxidermy in the purest sense of the word, it does permit the presentation of specimens such as worms, caterpillars, snakes and other small creatures which ordinarily would present quite a few technical problems due to their size.

Stated briefly, freeze-drying is a method of freezing the specimens to be displayed and then dehydrating them in a special chamber.

The specimens, which may be small creatures, plants or fungi, are first mounted and positioned using wire, sand and fillers. They are then frozen and transferred to the vacuum chamber which is usually part of the same equipment used for freezing.

The drying, which takes place over a period of days, causes an almost negligible amount of shrinkage. This is a distinct advantage over regular taxidermy. During the drying, the specimens are weighed weekly until no further loss of weight occurs. They are then removed from the chamber to the showcase.

Some types of small animals and birds benefit from a small amount of post-drying treatment. Some may require degreasing in an oil solvent, while others will benefit from plastic infiltration. This is accomplished in a vacuum bell jar with epoxy resin. The specimen is then embedded in clear epoxy casting.

Although the foregoing is a very brief outline, if it sounds as if it could be a spare-time project which appeals to you, further information may be obtained from some of the larger museums across the country. A very full account of the process may be found in **Popular Mechanics, Dec. 1969.**

The equipment used for freeze-drying may be bought ready for immediate use, but if you have the skill and inclination, you may prefer to make you own. Bear in mind, though, that the size and number of specimens to be treated is limited only by the size of the equipment.

The spare-time steps which you take to your first million are the ones which may be followed by anyone. The opportunities are there. All you have to do is grab hold of one.

TENT REPAIRS AND WATERPROOFING

Perhaps the outdoor life is one that appeals to you. Every year, thousands of Americans pack their car with a tent, sleeping bags, camp stove and all the essentials to camping in comfort, and take off for the green fields yonder.

It doesn't take much imagination to realize that there are thousands and thousands of tents scattered across the country, some in regular use, others stored away in garages and attics awaiting a time of renewed interest.

Many of the tents, especially those which are used frequently, are in a state of disrepair. This is a strange fact because new tents are expensive and the materials for renovating them are readily obtainable. The truth would seem to be that either people simply cannot be bothered or they are unaware of how easy it is to do minor repairs and waterproofing.

For someone with a little initiative and willingness to spend some of that spare time earning money, it's time to get started.

How to Get Started

Most tents require periodic waterproofing and repair. Actually, the term waterproofing is a misnomer because the tent material must be allowed to breathe without becoming porous.

First, the tent should be set up and examined for stains, tears and worn spots. Damage is frequently caused by twigs, sharp stones, bird droppings and mildew.

In the case of tears and rips, repairs may be effected by patching a piece of matching canvas over the damaged area. Experience will tell you whether this is best carried out with cement or stitching, or a combination of the two.

Ropes may need to be replaced and aluminum poles bent back into shape or replaced. When tents are badly damaged, whole sides may need replacing. The material for this may be obtained from Webb Manufacturing Co., Fourth at Gambia, Philadelphia, Pennsylvania.

Waterproofing may be carried out using the commercial tent waterproofing compounds supplied by stores which specialize in camping supplies. Generally, silicon or fluorocarbon waterproofing solutions cost more than the "oil treated" paraffin, but are far superior both for weight and performance. Instructions for using the waterproofing agent are usually supplied with the preparation.

The best way of getting business in this field is by local advertising. There may be areas in which there is no competition and it might be worthwhile to advertise in one or more of the camping journals. However, you would have to add freight charges to your cost for time and materials which may make out-of-state repairs an uneconomical proposition. This aspect of the business would depend on the current costs of freight and the cost of buying a new tent. Only an up-to-date review of costs would guide the direction of your advertising.

Closely allied to camping and hiking is the hobby of rock collecting. If you find pleasure in the search for unusual rocks and gemstones, there are many ways in which this may be turned into profit.

HOW TO TURN ROCKS INTO DIAMONDS

The attraction of rocks is almost irresistible. Few of us can stroll along a beach without pausing to pick up a pebble that has caught our eye. Rock polishing has become the hobby of people both young and old.

If rock hounding is your hobby, you are probably already aware of many of the ways in which you could turn your spare time into cash with rocks and gemstones as the center of your business. But if so far you have only toyed with the idea, now is the time to get started.

If rocks are only of passing interest, you are about to discover some of their attraction and ways in which you can convert that attraction into a hefty spare-time income.

How to Get Started

If you really turn your mind loose in this field, the possibilities of making money are enormous—to such an extent that it is difficult to select any specific areas to use as examples.

So, for the sake of convenience, we will divide this section into three categories; but they are only a fraction of the opportunities which await anyone with an active mind and an interest in gems and minerals.

1. Moneymaking with rough materials.
2. Simple steps in polished gems for the beginner.
3. Jewelry making for the advanced amateur.

Rocks in the rough state have been used as decorative materials for a long time. Fireplace surrounds, driveway entrances, walls and pillars. Small chippings of rock, or even weathered pebbles from the beach are being used to decorate room interiors and as material for the construction of table lamps, patio tables and planters.

The rock chippings may be bought very cheaply from quarries or garden landscaping companies. How you use them is bounded only by your imagination. If you look around you, it will become apparent that rocks and pebbles may be used for decoration embedded in either concrete or resin, and the objects so decorated have a high market value.

Vince G. bought a load of polished black pebbles and used them to surface his driveway by smoothing them into a layer of cement. After he had finished, he found himself with a quantity of unused material, so he used it to fashion square planters which he placed at the entrance to his driveway.

The planters he made were simple in construction. He made a sturdy wooden box, the inside dimensions of which were the ultimate size he needed. He then made a second box, smaller than the first, the difference in size being sufficient to put one box within the other, leaving enough space around the sides in which to pour pebbles and cement. By nailing two strips of wood across the top of the smaller box, he could suspend the smaller box inside the larger so that the top edges were level, and in this way provide space beneath the smaller box as he had at the sides. From that point on, it was merely a matter of mixing the cement and pebbles and pouring them into the space between the two boxes.

The planters aroused such favorable comment among the neighbors that he ordered a further small supply of pebbles and cement, and proceeded to make a series of planters which he placed along the front of his house.

So many friends and neighbors began asking him to make planters for them that Vince eventually began designing and making planters of pebble and rock as a spare-time business. Today he is making 200 planters a week in his spare time. His material costs him approximately 7¢ per planter and he sells the finished product at prices ranging from $2.50 to $12.00.

There are so many ways in which unfinished rock chippings may be used as decoration, that a full description is unnecessary. Just look around you at what is already being done and then let your imagination soar.

Polished gems are growing in popularity every day. Precious stones such as diamonds, rubies and emeralds have always commanded high prices. Recently, however, there has been a rising surge of interest in the less precious stones. Lapis lazuli, turquoise and opal are very popular and people are beginning to turn more to jasper, agate, garnet and amethyst.

If these semi-precious stones interest you and you feel you would enjoy working with them, there are numerous opportunities in the field of custom-made jewelry.

HOW TO GET STARTED IN THE FIELD OF
CUSTOM-MADE JEWELRY

Starting in a small way, you can buy polished gemstones in a wide variety of shapes and sizes, cut from some of the more popular minerals. Stores that specialize in gems and minerals can show you a selection sufficient to fill all your requirements. The magazine **Gems and Minerals** lists a great number of these stores across the country. The same stores will also supply a large variety of gem settings in the form of rings, pendants, bracelets, tie pins and earrings.

Although the cut gemstones can cost as little as $2 or $3 and the settings from $5, the finished jewelry will allow you more than 400 percent profit with friends and neighbors as first customers. If your work is tasteful and reasonably priced, word of mouth will supply you with all the customers you need.

As you become more professional, you may prefer to buy your gems wholesale from such countries as Australia, Pakistan and Brazil. The names and addresses of exporters in these and other countries may be found in **Gems and Minerals**.

Finally, if you are well advanced in this hobby, the opportunities for making money will hardly need explaining. Apart from the craft of ring designing and manufacturing, there are all the other applications of rock cutting and polishing. Objects such as bookends, clock surrounds, desk sets, ash trays and plant holders are only a few of a very long list.

The rough, coarse appearance of a geode or a piece of unpolished petrified wood may be a long way from the brilliance of a large diamond in a well-designed setting, but a well-planned venture into the rock business could give you a bank balance that will bring you all the diamonds you could wish for.

From the beauty of diamonds and emeralds, we now examine gems of a different kind—The beauty of miniature trees. Trees that are worth so much that only the very wealthy can buy them.

MONEYMAKING SECRETS OF
MINIATURE TREES

The graceful form of miniature trees has decorated the homes of Japan for several generations. Many of these tiny trees have been handed down from family to family, each caring for the plant with a reverence reserved for the very precious.

These miniature trees, known as ming trees or bonsai become more valuable as they grow older. Their owners train them and prune them into formal or semi-formal styles.

As these attractive, living works of art have become popular in countries outside of Japan, Jananese gardeners have begun growing bonsai especially for export. It is a big money business, but it is also one in which you can become involved.

How to Get Started

If you have any artistic inclinations at all, this surely must be one of the most satisfying of all hobbies. As with so many other spare-time ventures, begin by spending an hour or two in your public library. There are not too many books published on the growing of bonsai, but all you really need to know is the different types of plant which are particularly suited to bonsai culture. Plants which you will see illustrated may include: juniper, Chinese elm, chrysanthemum, ginkgo, azalea and pine.

There are many other plants which may be grown as bonsai, and of those mentioned, certain varieties adapt better than others. If the books you read do not provide sufficient information on the types of plants, it takes only a comparatively small amount of experimenting to discover which plants suit you the most. If you are going to make big money quickly with bonsai, there is one very important piece of information which you must know and understand.

The traditional bonsai, let's call it a miniature tree for the moment, is a fully mature tree which has been painstakingly pruned and trained over a period of many years until it has assumed an attractive style of growth.

It is impossible for you to make money **quickly** by growing a "true" bonsai. But what exactly is a "true" bonsai? It would appear to be a miniature tree of considerable age. In fact, and of most importance as far as you are concerned in your quest for that first million dollar smile from your bank manager, **bonsai can be of any age.** It is the appearance of the tree, the way it is pruned and shaped, and the way in which it is planted that makes it a bonsai.

It was knowing and fully understanding this fact that got Ron L. well on his way to a six figure bank balance. He first became interested in bonsai trees when his daughter bought him an imported juniper for his 50th birthday. Although his interest in gardening was only perfunctory, the tiny tree proved to be so attractive that he began to take an interest in its cultivation. Every week he would carefully prune the new growth and check to see that the training wires were correctly set.

With his new interest going full blast, Ron began noticing the bonsai plants being sold in the larger nurseries, but the high prices of the tiny trees deterred him from buying another plant. His interest was such that he decided to try growing his own bonsai trees. He began by buying three one gallon Chinese juniper plants from his local nursery. They were twisted and misshapen, spurned by the householder buying plants for his garden; but for the purpose Ron had in mind they were ideal specimens. They cost him $2.49 each.

From the same nursery Ron bought three bonsai dishes, rectangular earthenware plant pots about two inches deep. These dishes had been imported from Japan, and a little to Ron's consternation, cost him $9 each. But he knew they would provide the "authentic" bonsai look.

Working from directions in a book that he obtained from the public library, Ron cut away all the unnecessary branches very much in the way that a sculptor removes unwanted clay or chips away from unwanted wood or marble.

Within a few hours, Ron had three attractive miniature trees, each bent and wired in aesthetically pleasing shapes. They had the appearance of old, windswept trees.

Ron was pleased with his efforts, but when one of his friends remarked on the elegance they gave to his dining room and then added, "They must have set you back a bundle. I know how much those little trees cost," Ron began considering the possibility of making bonsai trees for sale.

The cost of his venture would include plants, soil, planters, and copper wire. To these continuing costs, he decided to add a $35 initial investment for special pruning shears and trowel.

Ron quickly found ways to reduce manufacturing costs. Instead of buying plants one or two at a time from the local nursery, he opened an account with a large, wholesale grower, and by purchasing 25 plants at a time, reduced the average price for each plant from $2.50 down to $1.25.

The potting soil was sufficiently inexpensive in 50 lb. sacks, and instead of buying the copper wire from the local hardware store, he found he could buy exactly what he needed from a scrap metal dealer. It came in the form of insulated electrical wire, and when stripped of the insulation and passed through the flame of a blow torch, it filled the need exactly.

At first, the pots or dishes proved a problem. Ron could either buy them directly from the dealer, try to discover the wholesaler or importer or, as a last resort, try to import them himself from Japan. The solution proved to be none of these alternatives and was so obvious he wondered why he didn't think of it earlier.

Ron visited a nearby college and made a few enquiries of the ceramics teacher. Within a week Ron had been put in touch with a local woman, a bank teller, whose spare-time hobby was ceramics. She agreed to supply him with bonsai dishes almost identical to the Japanese originals.

This arrangement proved to have two advantages over importing dishes from Japan. First, there was never any hold up in supplies; and second, the homecrafted dishes were 25 percent cheaper than the Japanese version.

The only part of Ron's venture where he had anticipated any real difficulties, the selling of the bonsai, proved to present no problems at all. Almost without exception, every retail nursery to which Ron offered his bonsai, wanted to stock them. In addition to these eager outlets, Ron sold some of his more elaborate efforts directly to the public by advertisements in the local paper and by displays at fairs and home and garden exhibitions.

When he first started selling his bonsai, the plants which cost him an average of $5 including the planter, were selling to the retailer for $10 who then sold them to the public at prices in excess of $25 each.

Today, some of Ron's plants bring him more than $250 each and he has four young women helping him to keep up with the demand. At present, Ron is planning to start holding classes once a week to teach people the art of growing miniature trees.

Ron had discovered that hobbies and pastimes have a very high profit potential. Almost every sport or hobby can lead you to immense wealth. Take hunting, for example.

SPECIALIZED FIREARM SERVICES

It has been estimated that one in every four homes throughout the United States of America houses a firearm. Sometimes it is a handgun tucked away in a drawer or hidden under the mattress—a gun owned purely for protection and probably never ever fired. At other times it could be a rifle or a shotgun, carefully chosen and used specifically for hunting game birds or animals.

Then there is that clearly defined group with very expensive, highly accurate rifles who use their weapons for competitive target shooting. Within this group would also be the more casual sportsman who spends a few hours at the weekend trap shooting.

The man or woman with mechanical aptitude and an interest in firearms can very quickly establish a profitable spare-time business. The steps this time must lead to specialization—the specialist who can clean, repair, adjust and align almost any type of firearm.

The market is already well-established. All that is necessary is to convince the owners of those weapons that they need your very special service.

How to Get Started

Let's take the first group and explore ways of promoting your service. These are the people who have a firearm purely for protection. Many people in this group have never fired a rifle or handgun and in most cases, fervently hope they never have to. But how many of those weapons are safe? How many could be more dangerous to the user than to the intruder?

An advertisement in a local newspaper exposing the dangers of a faulty weapon and offering a thorough cleaning and inspection for a nominal sum will almost certainly bring business. That nominal sum will frequently be augmented where repairs are found to be necessary and proposed.

The second group, the hunters, need a weapon which is completely reliable. While most of these people clean and cherish their weapons, only a few have the tools, knowledge and time to carry out repairs.

Again, an advertisement which offers to maintain hunting equipment at its maximum efficiency will bring considerable response. Further profit within this group can come from offering hand-loaded shells prepared to individual specifications.

The third group, the marksmen, is probably the most exacting of the three and because of this, the one most prepared to pay well for professional services. For this group you must offer and supply just two unquestionable results—efficiency and accuracy.

A first-rate service will provide you with a reputation no advertising could ever achieve. The best way to reach members of this group is either by direct mail or through an advertisement placed in the clubhouse or, where it exists, through the club's newsletter.

All through this chapter the emphasis has been on hobbies and pastimes which appeal to you. When you have an interest in any subject, it follows that you also have knowledge on that subject. That knowledge can be the spare-time opportunity you have been seeking.

HOW TO CONVERT YOUR KNOWLEDGE INTO DOLLARS

Most people have a hobby or pastime. It is almost a certainty that you have one. There are a few individuals who have no interests other than working, eating and sleeping (even eating can be more than simply a necessity, ask a gourmet). But such people are rare and given a chance, even those who would at first believe they have no interest in recreational activities will admit to at least owning a camera.

There is a fortune to be made at every turn of the road. Hobbies and pastimes lend themselves very readily to "the money game," and it's up to you to plan and prepare. You are the sole master of your own destiny. Don't wait for someone to come along and thrust a six figure check into your hand. It won't happen. The check is there, just waiting for you, but you have to go and get it.

How to Get Started

Start by talking to yourself. Ask yourself exactly what your hobbies and interests are, then decide precisely what you know about them. The extent of your knowledge is much greater than you think. You may consider grabbing a pencil and paper to make a list of the things you know about your hobby.

Save your time and energy. When you get down to it, you'll find you have enough knowledge to write a whole book. Now there's an idea! If you've got the slightest gift for words, why not write a book based on your personal knowledge of any particular leisure field? Or if you think writing a book may be a bit ambitious to start with, why not try your hand at an article or two? Magazines pay well for knowledgeable articles, especially if they are illustrated with one or two photographs.

When you really examine the extent of your knowledge, you'll discover that there are many areas which, with a little thought, can be turned into large amounts of cash.

It is obviously impossible to provide illustrations from your field of knowledge. Only you know what you know and only you can decide the best way of cashing in on that knowledge. But to give you an idea of the possibilities, here are a couple of examples of knowledge turning into a substantial spare-time income.

David N. was an oil engineering consultant, but his hobby was butterfly collecting. The results of many years and many visits to foreign countries were housed in the cabinets and drawers that lined his study.

Eventually, his collection was so complete that new specimens were added fairly infrequently. Gradually, his interest began to turn to breeding some of the more rare specimens— a feat achieved by only a handful of people.

The knowledge that David had accumulated through his patience and perseverance is paying off in pleasure and hard cash. His butterflies, or at least the cocoons, are sold to collectors, schools and museums all over the world.

Jim B. provides the other example of knowledge that earns an income. By profession, Jim is a natural fuels consultant, but wherever he travels he relaxes with music. His radio is always tuned to those stations which broadcast popular music. Almost subconsciously, Jim found he could unerringly spot new tunes which would zoom to the top of the hit charts.

One day while travelling by plane from Los Angeles to Washington, Jim found himself sitting next to an executive of one of the top music companies. Naturally, the top tunes of the day became a topic of conversation.

When Jim mentioned his ability to spot winners almost before they were written, his traveling companion challenged him to pick out three tunes which would reach the number one position. Without hesitation, Jim mentioned three song titles. Three months later, after each of the forecasts proved accurate, Jim received a letter from the executive offering an interesting proposition.

Every two months, the recording company would send him a tape containing several recent recordings not yet publicly aired. They would pay him $500 if he would pick out the tune or tunes destined for success. If he made no mistakes in six months, they offered to retain him as a spare-time public opinion consultant with a retainer of $2,000 a month.

In three years, Jim has only missed once. The tune he selected on that occasion only reached number two on the charts. The recording company continues to be well-satisfied. Armed with Jim's knowledgeable forecasts they reinforce their own judgment on which way to allocate their advertising budget.

Knowledge is always potential wealth. They say that "What you don't know won't hurt you," but a better saying might be, "What you know can make you a millionaire." Nowhere is this more true than in the field of collecting.

Chapter 8

How to Make Big Money in the Big Interest Field of Collecting

Just about anything is collectable—the interesting and the uninteresting, the old and the very new. Collectors may be seen browsing in antique shops, wandering thoughtfully through "swap meets" or spending a weekend scavenging at places resembling the sites of long abandoned gold mines. The finds these people make are sometimes almost as valuable as a gold mine in full production.

If you are by nature one of those individuals who hates to throw anything away, collecting might be just your cup of tea. Better still, it could be your means of amassing a considerable fortune.

HOW TO GET STARTED

Collecting sometimes seems to start almost accidentally. The stamp on a letter from a foreign country is too pretty to throw away, so you tear it from the envelope and drop it in that old cookie jar in the cupboard. When this has happened several times a collection has started.

The collection becomes a fact at spring cleaning time when the jar is taken from the cupboard and a firm decision has to be made whether to continue collecting those pretty stamps or to throw them away. The old habit wins out and a collection is on its way. After all, if you found it difficult to throw one stamp away, it is much more difficult to dispose of an entire collection, no matter how small.

The same thing applies to the more common collectables: coins, matchboxes and figurines. But sometimes manufacturers put out a new product and announce it to be the beginning of a series with a limited number of pieces to be produced. Hallmark did this with their beautifully crafted Christmas ornaments. Hummel produces plates, figurines and Christmas ornaments which are much sought-after collector's items. At the time of this writing, comedian Red Skelton has produced the first plate of an intended series depicting his paintings of clowns—a collection which is certain to be very much in demand.

Collecting, therefore, becomes something you do because it gives you pleasure. Whether you slide into it gently and unknowingly, or whether it is a conscious decision prompted by someone else's collection or through a manufacturer's advertising; collecting is an occupation—spare-time or full-time—which can be so strong as to become an obsession.

With a subject so strong and at times compulsive, it is inevitable that someone is going to reap huge profits. That someone may as well be you.

If you are not already into collecting but feel that this field is one which would interest you, it's time to take those first steps. Begin by making a list of all the types of collections of which you are already aware, regardless of whether you know anything about the subject or not. Knowledge can be gained as you go.

Some of the first types of collections to come to mind will be coins, stamps, objets d' art, paintings, butterflies and books. Look into it a lot more closely and you will start discovering a new world of interests.

There are people who collect bottles—usually very old bottles, regardless of their previous contents. There are other people who collect only wine and liquor bottles. There are collections of old type barbed wire, old nails, electrical insulators, door handles, newspaper clippings, pressed flowers, family portraits, model airplanes, model cars, old automobiles, wartime medals, regiment insignias, dolls, gravestone rubbings and rare gems.

When you think you've exhausted all the possibilities, you can start grinding all those subjects into still finer grain. For instance, you could specify that all the door handles had to be glass or, if you prefer, brass. You could insist that you would collect regiment insignias from a certain period of time, say, the Civil War, or from a certain country. The possibilities are endless.

There are many opportunities staring you in the face and many choices of steps toward your first six figure bank balance. All you have to do is to decide which one you'd like to tackle. It isn't even essential that you tackle just one. You could very well tackle a dozen different subjects at the same time. If you find you can't get along with the one you've chosen, you simply drop it and start on a new one.

Easy money? You bet. Big money? Without a doubt! If you are wondering exactly how to get into this fabulous gold mine, read on. It would be impossible to detail every type of collection, but the next six sections will provide you with enough information for you to found your own very profitable spare-time business.

BIG MONEY IN THE COIN MARKET

Every coin ever made has a value. The coins you jangle in your pocket or purse have a value; usually the one stated on the coin—the face value. While some people do collect this type of coin, doing so isn't always a profitable venture.

If you need proof of this, imagine putting away in a box exactly enough money to buy, say, ten gallons of gasoline or perhaps two pairs of shoes. Leave the money untouched for five years and then see how many gallons of gasoline and how many pairs of shoes it will buy.

The lesson is obvious and yet there are coins which not only leap in value year after year, but are in fact absolutely safe forms of saving.

No matter what the economic condition is of the country in which you live, carefully selected coins will always have a ready market if you wish to sell them. There is always, somewhere in the world, a wealthy collector who will buy what you have to offer, especially if what you have to offer is rare. In that previous sentence is the whole essence of collecting—rarity.

There are really only two ways of getting hold of rare coins. The first way is to buy them, either from a coin dealer, at an auction or from a private collector.

The second way is to watch the coins which pass through your hands every day and armed with knowledge of what to look for, start your collection in this way. The disadvantages of this second method of getting started are obvious. Your collection would be founded on time, knowledge and luck.

The knowledge can be gathered from one of half a dozen books which list rare coins in circulation. Coins such as an 1873-CC quarter which in fine condition would be worth in excess of $250. A 1973-CC with arrows in fine condition would be worth more than $300. Coins such as these are rare because there are only a few in circulation, usually because only a comparatively small number were minted.

For example, a quarter dated 1896-S would be worth about $100. There were 188,039 minted, but the 1896-0 in similar condition would be worth only $7. Of these, 1,484,000 were minted.

In watching for coins which pass through your hands, time and luck go hand in hand. You can do very little about either, therefore your collection will be governed by the whims of chance. Who knows? Perhaps the very day you read this, you'll go through the pennies in your piggy bank and find a cent dated 1877. It's worth more than $100, providing that it's in fine condition.

If you are not prepared to let the laws of chance play too great a part in your spare-time moneymaking endeavors and you would like to make coins the basis of your venture, you will have to resort to buying the coins you need.

But before you start investing any money at all, make yourself completely familiar with the business (and it really is a business), of coin collecting. Read every book you can that deals with the subject of coins and coin collecting. Study the magazines which deal with coin collecting. Not just the current issues, but copies which date back at least five years.

Watch for trends. Take a note of the coins which increase in value steadily and suspect the big, spectacular sales. Watch for the minting of special coins and, as happened recently, coins that have been stored away in a vault for many years and are suddenly brought to light and sold by auction.

There is money to be made in coin collecting, but the really successful collector is the person who has a thorough knowledge of the subject. Anyone can gain knowledge, it's not something only obtainable by the wealthy. Nor is it something only known to the poor. Your race and sex play no part in the gathering of knowledge, but you have to make the effort.

Knowledge can bring you huge dividends in another similar field—the field of postage stamps.

DOLLAR BILLS AND OLD ENVELOPES

There is an undeniable fascination about postage stamps. To the uninitiated they come in many shapes and quite often they are decorated with colorful pictures.

The enthusiast will tell you that they are miniature masterpieces of art. They depict the political trends of a country, they teach geography, they have historical significance and they are often worth considerable amounts of money.

If you have an interest in what is surely the king of collections (philately) and would like to make money at the same time, there is no better time to get started than now.

How to Get Started

Collecting stamps can be as easy as walking into a dime store and putting your money on the counter. All you need is an album and some stamps to place in it, and you've become a stamp collector. Now the question is, where's the big money? Well, it's not to be found in the dime store. At least, not in the way you think. But we'll come back to that later.

If you've read through the previous chapters, you know exactly where your first stop is going to be. That's right, the public library. In the library you will find many books dealing with stamp collecting. You will find books devoted to certain types of stamps, books which deal with stamps by the country of their origin and books which tell you in great detail exactly how to

collect stamps and how to get the greatest pleasure from collecting.

On the same shelf in the library, you will find catalogues
which list every stamp ever printed together with their current
market value. These catalogues are going to be your working bi-
ble. If you are going into the stamp business, it would be worth
your while to purchase a complete catalogue for your reference
shelf.

While you are in the library, don't neglect to study the
magazines dealing with the hobby and don't overlook the young
people's department. Some remarkably instructive books may
be found in the children's section.

From this fountain of knowledge you will soon discover
that certain stamps, the rarer ones, are worth many hundreds
of dollars. Sometimes, when those stamps are still attached to
postmarked envelopes, they are worth considerably more.

Now, at this point, you should refer back to the previous section. Everything that was said about coins could equally well be
said about stamps. In this section, however, we will amplify the
possibilities a little more as they apply to making money with
postage stamps.

There are dealers throughout the world who specialize in
the selling of stamps in bulk. Their names and addresses may
always be found in the advertising section of the philately
magazines. These dealers collect stamps from many sources.
Private collections, boy scout door-to-door canvassing, church
donations, bankruptcy sales and so on.

To a large extent, especially when so advertised, these bulk
offerings are unsorted. You may find in any of these bulk buys,
stamps of considerable value. To make this deal even more
interesting and attractive, these bulk parcels are at ridiculously low prices. But there are three snags. First, the bulk parcels
contain a great many stamps that are almost worthless.

Second, you are faced with the task of sorting these stamps,
pricing them from the catalogue and, in many instances,

removing them from torn wrapping paper or sections of envelopes.

Third, because you are buying in bulk, the initial outlay will cost you $25, $50, $100 or $500, depending on the size parcel you decide to purchase.

Here is where the bulk parcels can pay big dividends. Apart from the very real possibility of discovering rare and valuable stamps (one stamp could conceivably bring you more than the entire cost of the parcel), all those duplicates and less expensive stamps can be sold in several ways.

1. You can sort and mount them in small folder albums and offer them for sale as "approvals." The quickest way to find out how the approval system works, is to answer one of the advertisements offering approvals. You will find advertisements offering approvals in almost every major newspaper and many magazines.

2. You can repackage and sell your unwanted stamps in smaller bulk parcels, offering clean and sorted stamps. (No rare stamps, but a lot for your money.)

3. As a third alternative, you can sort your stamps into various types of categories—categories such as: triangular stamps; stamps that depict animals, flowers, sports, famous buildings, butterflies, anniversaries, etc.

These collections, comprising perhaps two, five, ten or more stamps, can be packaged and sold either directly to the public or, and here we are back to the dime store, through any retail outlet which is prepared to display a selection of postage stamps.

In the latter instance your packaging would have to be attractive and, for this type of merchandising, you may wish to consult one of the packaging design businesses to be found in the yellow pages of most telephone directories.

The stamp collecting business is an easy one to enter. It is a type of merchandise with which the public is very familiar and you are not faced with the problem of promoting your merchandise. Only your name and service need promotion.

Moving away from the familiar and traveling in the opposite direction, there are still further opportunities waiting for you. Opportunities for you to earn sufficient money in your spare time to become financially sound for the rest of your life. Steps that can take you into the world of unlimited wealth.

TREMENDOUS PROFITS FROM THE UNUSUAL

You can sell absolutely anything. If you have a burning desire to be very wealthy, to be able to buy anything your heart desires, you can sell anything. If there is enough money to be made, you'd sell refrigerators to Eskimos (it's been done), or high fashion to Aborigines (that's been done too) or sand to Arabs (and that as well).

But why take on difficult sales when there is a tremendous market for items which are all around you? Providing you know where, how, and what, the variety of items you can sell is unlimited.

How to Get Started

For this type of spare-time venture, you have to develop a watchful eye and the ability to put one and one together and arrive correctly at two.

Once you get the idea and the habit of smart thinking, you'll start making money every time you step outside your front door. It's all a matter of providing a very special kind of service and this is how it works.

On her way to work every morning, Betty R. watched a housing development gradually taking shape. She was slightly amused by the pile of toilets carefully stacked to one side of the lot. Nobody seemed interested in installing them in the houses as they reached completion.

Her interest quickened one morning when she noticed a second consignment of toilets had been delivered and stacked some

distance from the first batch. Now there were obviously far too
many toilets for the number of houses. Curiosity was getting the
better of her, so she stopped and asked one of the workmen why
there were so many. He told her that the first batch was found to
have faulty base moldings which made them difficult to seal.
They were due to be scrapped.

Betty asked for the name of the manufacturer and wrote to
him offering $100 for all of the faulty toilets. There were 50
altogether. The manufacturer, faced with the prospect of
having to re-ship them simply to have them scrapped, replied
that she could have them for $100 providing she arranged her
own transportation.

She took them back to her house, four at a time in her station
wagon and stacked them in her backyard. Her next step was to
have a local upholsterer make a small padded cover for one of
the plastic seat tops. The sample cost Betty $6.

When this was ready, she made an appointment and took the
toilet to a nightclub on the other side of town. There she talked
with the owner and showed him her sample. He agreed to buy all
her toilets for $500 without the padded cover. He said he would
arrange his own upholstering using fabrics to suit his decor.

Betty had put one and one together. On a previous visit to
the nightclub, Betty had been introduced to the owner and he
had mentioned that he intended to open another restaurant or
nightclub, but he was looking for an idea to make it different—
to the point of being bizarre. He wanted his restaurant to be the
most talked about place in town.

When Betty showed him her sample and suggested that instead of conventional seating, each table should be equipped
with colorfully upholstered toilets, the restaurant owner knew
it was exactly the gimmick for which he was looking.

Betty had calculated that she was not overreaching when
she bought the faulty toilets. If this restaurant owner had not
wanted them, she was confident that she could sell the idea to
some other progressive restaurateur.

A small chain of grocery stores on the West coast is using a number of old traffic signals flashing a green light as an attention grabber. They were sold to the chain by one of their customers. Many bars and resaurants in the center of large towns, miles from the sea, have old ship's wheels, fishing nets, ship's bells and lanterns as interior decor. These items may be picked up very cheaply in old ship repair yards.

Look around you as you go about your daily chores and once your eyes become trained to spot good buys, it's only a matter of bringing the two together.

People are always seeking the unusual and the rare. For as long as there are collectors, there will be someone who will sell to those collectors. At this very moment you may have in your attic or garage a pile of dollar bills that you were just considering giving to the trash collector.

A TREASURE HOUSE OF MAGAZINES
AND PAPERBACKS

Magazines have always been collector's items. Many collections of magazines are in the possession of people who are not even aware that they are collectors.

It happens like this. A man or woman becomes interested in a subject, say, solar energy, so they take out a subscription to a magazine, perhaps **Popular Science**, which publishes up to the minute information on that subject.

Over a period of time, that interest in solar energy may wane, but by then the magazine has become a continuing source of pleasure. Articles on other subjects contain information which may be of use at a future date so the magazines are retained, sometimes to be bound in 12 monthly binders.

For some reason hard to explain, certain magazines become greatly sought after. Early issues in good condition bring very high prices. **Playboy** is such a magazine, and so is

Saturday Evening Post. Collectors endeavor to obtain a copy of every issue published. Where there are gaps in those collections, the collectors are forever watchful for an opportunity to obtain the missing issues.

Where do they look for these back issues? At swap meets, garage sales, church bazaars, rummage sales and thrift stores. They also periodically visit stores which specialize in buying and selling used books and magazines.

How to Get Started

At this point you are beginning to know precisely how to move in on opportunities such as this. On one side is the market—a hungry market which you can enter—and on the other side is an almost unlimited supply of merchandise.

Where do you obtain this merchandise? From exactly those same sources which the collectors explore. However, you are out to make money and the collectors are merely trying to fill gaps in their collections. Here is how to turn your endeavors into dollar bills.

As with most businesses, you will have to make an initial investment. But if you approach this type of venture correctly, that investment will be surprisingly small.

Your first step is to ascertain which magazines are the ones most sought after. The easiest way to gain this information is by watching newspaper classified advertisements or by taking a trip to a store which sells used magazines.

There are not too many of these stores, but most large cities have at least one. The prices and scarcity of certain magazines will give you a sure guide to the collector's items. Don't overlook comic books in your search for collectables.

Armed with the knowledge of the types of magazines you need, your next step is to buy these magazines in quantity and at a low price. The best place to buy in this way is from garage sales, swap meets and rummage sales. Never be afraid to make an offer for all the magazines being offered. Quite often a householder cleaning house and holding a garage sale will put out perhaps 50 magazines at 10¢ or 25¢ each.

At 10¢ each they would expect to get $5 if they sold all the magazines. But bearing in mind that their primary objective is to clear junk from the house, they will usually be pleased to accept your offer of $1 or $2 for all of the magazines.

Gradually, your stock of magazines and comics will grow, and the bigger selection you have to offer, the more you will sell—but not at 10¢ or 25¢ each. The more rare and sought after magazines can bring as much as $200 or $300 each.

Even the not-so-rare issues will bring at least half the original publishing price and, at times, two or three times that amount when sold to collectors still in the early stages of gathering their collection. The easiest way to sell your merchandise is by means of classified advertising, offering rare and hard-to-find magazines.

Working along the same lines, it is easy and comparatively inexpensive to assemble an extremely comprehensive library of paperback books.

Nancy G. has transformed the walls of her garage with floor to ceiling shelves filled with row after row of paperbacks. All the books are carefully arranged in categories of fiction and non-fiction with crime, western, science fiction, romance and adventure in the fiction section; and cooking, psychology, travel, education, self help, gardening, etc., in the non-fiction section.

The prices range from 50¢ to $1 each, and although she is open for business only three evenings a week and all day Saturday, her profits are more than $100 a week. This is reasonable seeing that she started her business only two months ago.

Nancy says that her quick success is because she specializes. Steve B. also specializes in his spare-time venture, but his is the field of strange and beautiful gems.

WEALTH FROM GEMS AND MINERALS

Although gems and minerals were mentioned in the previous chapter, Steve B. has directed his interests into two very profitable channels.

Two years ago, 25-year-old Steve discovered one of the hard facts of life. It was no new, earth shaking fact, but it suddenly became important to Steve.

He worked for a while as a swimming pool salesman. His sales were very predictable. He sold three times as many pools in the wealthier part of town than he did in the less wealthy. When he began to develop his hobby of gem collecting and polishing into a spare-time business, he concentrated exclusively on the higher income areas.

Steve B. conceived the idea of decorating the collars of cats and dogs, and the harnesses of horses with polished gems. Sometimes the gems were birthstones, sometimes they were purely decorative gems chosen by the owners of the animals.

It wasn't long before Steve exhausted his collection of polished gems, and instead of spending valuable time in preparing a fresh supply of gemstones, he sought out other hobbyists and arranged to buy stones from them while he continued to seek further work and concentrated on carrying out that work as it came in.

Word of his skill spread, and orders flooded in. Steve was asked to decorate a wide variety of items apart from the harnesses and collars. Key rings, belts, sandals, wristwatch straps, and purses are among some of the items he is asked to decorate, and his reputation grows greater each day. Steve has exchanged his Ford for a Cadillac, his house has a new swimming pool and with a spare-time income of $1,500 a month, he can afford them.

Barbara T. saw her idea in a dream. She woke up and wrote it down on paper while it was still fresh in her mind, and then at the first opportunity, she turned the idea into reality. Hers was a simple craft item, startlingly beautiful, and it sold on sight. Within two years, working entirely in her spare time, Barbara has built her income up to $40,000 a year, has five people working for her, and sells through a distribution chain which is nationwide.

Briefly, Barbara's dream idea used two identical planters, one upside down and the other on top. The upside-down planter was decorated in a very original way. Originally, Barbara made her item of cheap, red clay flower pots, but as her business grew, she progressed to making her item of fired and decorative planters. Finally, she began having planters made to her special requirements.

Her innovative idea was to drill a pattern of tiny holes in one of the pots and insert small rhinestones into these holes. She then placed an electric light bulb holder with a 40 watt bulb beneath the inverted pot. The light, gleaming through the tiny gemstones, turned the flower pot into a beautiful table decoration. To complete her item, she planted a suitable indoor plant in the second pot and fastened it over the illuminated one.

The entire decorator's item cost Barbara between $4 and $6 to produce, depending on the type of pots she used. They sell in the stores for between $29.95 and $49.95. Barbara had turned a dream into a healthy, spare-time business.

Reg. R. works at a steel mill during the day. During the evening he spends his spare time slicing geodes from Mexico into two halves, cementing them to polished rock of various kinds and adding a small plaque which reads: Souvenir of Laguna Beach, Souvenir of San Francisco, Souvenir of Miami and so on. The souvenirs are distributed by a wholesaler of gift items with outlets in most of the major tourist centers.

If you are a collector of gems and minerals, there are many, many ways of making money through your knowledge of this hobby. It is all a matter of ideas and imagination.

Collections of all types are potential moneymakers. But more profitable than the collections themselves, is the knowledge gained in the collecting. That knowledge can make you rich.

CASH FROM COLLECTIONS FOR INTERIOR DECOR

Top among collections for interior decor, are original oil paintings. Seascapes, landscapes, portraits, scenes of the old West and animals are typical subjects to be found in almost any home, and there are artists who specialize in these and many other art themes.

These artists are easy to find, especially those who are up and coming. Visits to art schools and open air exhibitions will quickly lead you to the source of what is often some very interesting original art. Having found the source, you now need to know how to apply this knowledge to the gentle art of making money.

How to Get Started

Interior decorators are the foremost users of original art. By introducing yourself as an entrepreneur, you offer to provide the decorator with the type of art he or she requires.

The more successful decorators are fully engaged in meeting new clients, and carrying out or supervising the contracted work. Although some of the more progressive artists, sculptors and photographers approach the interior decorators personally in an effort to sell their work, there are many who are too involved in the production of that work to have time for the commercial aspects. So you offer to act as middleman.

Your profit in this type of enterprise will vary from 15 percent to 50 percent. If an artist wants $200 for a painting, you can either arrange to sell it to the decorator for $200 and take your percentage from the price asked by the artist or, if his price is firm, you add your percentage in your quotation to the decorator.

The tools you need for this type of work are knowledge, perseverance, a good camera and the skill to produce attractive pictures.

It would be impossible to carry around a car full of works of art, even if the artist would agree to you doing this. Consequently, the answer is an album of really attractive, selling pictures.

If you are not capable of taking pictures that sell products, have them taken by a commercial photographer. The artist will usually agree to pay this expense.

Now you are all set to go. As you gather momentum in this business, you'll find you can sell these interior decor items to institutions such as banks, museums, restaurants, hospitals, nursing homes, dentist and doctor offices, corporate offices and city halls. Then when you think you've exhausted all the possbilities, just look around you. Every private home is a potential customer.

Before leaving the subject of items for interior decoration, you should be aware that there are people who make a very high, spare-time income collecting and selling driftwood, manzanita wood, sea shells, old prints and pictures, animal head trophies, old advertising posters, hunting horns, engravings and pewter.

Restaurants and bars located close to an airport are usually good prospects for items such as World War I airplane propellers. Those located near sports stadiums, tennis clubs and golf courses will usually be very interested in autographed sports equipment.

If it's collectable it's sellable. It is all a matter of knowing what people want and calculating methods of supplying what is needed.

Chapter 9

How to Make Money in the Big Interest Field Of Organic Food

Food can be a really big money spinner. From the small delicatessen store at the corner of the street to the giant conglomerate of General Mills, food provides a never ending source of profit. The market potential is enormous and completely unlimited—everybody buys food.

The spare-time moneymaker who intends to get into the food business is entering a field where there's plenty of room for everyone. Your first spare-time step is to find the correct "angle" and decide which section of this tremendous market offers the greatest money making opportunities for you.

THE EXPANDING MARKET FOR ORGANIC FOOD

It has been calculated that for every 8,000 food items on the shelves of the supermarkets, 5,000 originated in the test tubes of biochemists. The public is at last beginning to protest and there is a growing demand for natural, organic food. This fast growing trend has created its own highly profitable market. It is a market tailor-made for the person determined to earn big money in his or her spare time.

The easiest and most obvious way to make money in organic food is to grow it and sell it. This could present a difficulty to the person living in an apartment in the center of town, but as you will see in a moment, there's more than one way to peel this organic orange.

When you're determined to take those steps which lead to the really big money, there's a solution to every problem. It's only those first few steps that sometimes seem insurmountable. Once you've acquired the knack of power thinking, you'll find those first few steps are not so difficult after all. The subsequent ones get easier and easier.

CHOOSING THE PRODUCT

Perhaps at this time we should determine exactly what is meant by the term "organic food." Strictly speaking, organic food is food that has not been contaminated with pesticides, has not been fertilized with chemical fertilizers and does not contain artificial sweeteners, colorings or preservatives.

Let's take a look at the foods to which the term "organic" applies, and then you can decide for yourself which ones interest you most. You should consider the advantages and disadvantages of each product as it applies to you personally, but be careful to examine each apparent disadvantage objectively.

You'll be surprised how often something which appears to be a major stumbling block can be turned or twisted to your personal benefit. The problem you solve may have already discouraged a potential competitor.

Foods which can be grown or produced organically include:

Vegetables	Fruit	Eggs
Meat	Bread	Jams and Marmalade
Herbs	Honey	Oils
Shortenings	Juices	Crackers and Cookies
Butter	Peanut Butter	Milk

In a book this size, it would be impossible to deal with each product exhaustively, but if we select one or two and explore the moneymaking possibilities, you'll soon understand how almost any food can be a straight, well-paved highway to your first million.

Keep in mind that your target is to become really wealthy as quickly and simply as possible. Look for the shortest route and avoid putting obstacles in your own path. Select a product which is practical and one which appeals to you.

GETTING STARTED

Let us consider the quickest way to get started in the business of organic food, assuming for the moment that you have a small patch of ground—even if it's only a corner of the backyard—that you can turn over to cultivation.

You may have already considered the possibility of growing fruit or vegetables to supplement your income. Although this is always a steady way to coin extra cash, there are ways to build market gardening into a spare-time business at a speed you would never have thought possible.

In order to reach the high income brackets fast and efficiently, you must have a carefully planned program. Give considerable thought to the type of produce you are going to market. Don't pick a certain fruit or vegetable just because you have a personal liking for it. Make your selection from produce which will give you the maximum annual crop and one assured of a steady consumer demand.

If you can market produce which is slightly rare or even exotic—produce such as greenhouse cucumbers, guavas, grapes, artichokes and nuts—so much the better. In this way your profit percentage will be higher than it would be for items in more plentiful supply.

But it is by using special marketing techniques, backed by sustained effort, that your bank balance will really start to expand. Here are seven ways to start your income growing. Use them to spark ideas of your own.

SEVEN PROVEN TECHNIQUES

1. Start by building a neighborhood clientele. For $20 you can have 1,000 two-color leaflets printed. Have them delivered door-to-door throughout your area. Make sure that they are delivered methodically—don't just haphazardly paper the town with them. Keep a check on the houses which receive your leaflets and follow-up a day or two later with a personal call.

It is important that your leaflets promote what you have to sell and state that you will be making regular deliveries in the neighborhood. They should also continually stress the word organic. When your product has an advantage over other products in the field, you cannot shout loud enough about that advantage.

2. Set your prices at the same level that the local supermarket has established for similar non-organic food. This will give you the desired advantage plus an adequate profit margin while you are getting your business under way.

3. Package your produce attractively. Plastic produce bags 10 by 12 inches cost approximately $3 per 1,000 and for just

a dollar or two more, you can have them overprinted with your name and a slogan.

Attractive packaging not only makes your product more appealing, but shows that you have a personal interest and pride in what you have to offer.

Make sure the word **organic** is printed as large as possible. Organic is the massive advantage you have over the bulk grower. Plug it for all you're worth.

4. When you make your follow-up calls, try to leave samples. Samples demonstrate, without you having to labor the point, that you are not afraid to have your product tested. Any experienced salesman will tell you that persuading your prospective customer to handle the merchandise is half the battle when making a sale.

5. Be friendly—even when you **get** impolite refusals. A neighbor may sell that refusal for you at a later date, but word of mouth recommendations are wasted if you have left a poor impression.

6. Increase the interest in your product by devising new recipes incorporating the type of produce you're selling. Have these recipes printed on the back of you business cards and use them as space fillers on your leaflets.

7. Try arranging periodic demonstrations. You'll be amazed how many people will accept an invitation to try new ideas in food. The dishes need not be very elaborate but they must be different.

Carol W. of San Diego held what she called an "organic food tasting party." The hit of the afternoon was organic greenhouse cucumbers, sliced thinly and placed between slices of buttered organic rye bread. The sandwiches were toasted on the outside and, after removed from the grill, opened and spread with organic cream cheese. This is simple and effective. Carol obviously considers that she is heading in the right direction. She recently started building her third greenhouse.

There are so many opportunities in organic food that you can literally lay the foundation stone of a major industry within the next two hours. Does that sound incredible? Why don't you try it and see for yourself? All you have to do is to turn to that tiny factory which is at the very root of the entire food industry—the home kitchen.

SPECIALIZED KITCHEN PRODUCTS

Many men and women who now enjoy a life of comfort and security started their climb to wealth in the kitchen of their own home.

Mrs. Cordelia Knott, together with her husband, started a small home based business with a roadside berry stand, selling jellies and preserves from her kitchen. Today, the million dollar Knott's Berry Farm competes strongly with the giant Disneyland to provide attractions to southern California.

Mrs. Banuello expanded her homemade tortillas into the huge Ramona Mexican Food Corporation before turning her business skills to politics by accepting the position of Secretary to the Treasury of the United States.

You too can start with a simple idea and withing an amazingly short time, watch it grow into a huge million dollar business.

HOW SIMPLICITY PAYS OFF

The whole success formula is built from one word—simplicity. The trend towards organic food is growing at relentless speed. There is a turning away from all the complexities and subterfuges of modern processed food. Take a step back in time in order to take many giant financial strides forward. Begin by searching old-fashioned cookbooks for those good old mouthwatering meals.

Perhaps you have a favorite recipe that has been handed down from mother to daughter in your family. Many of those old time recipes are now proving to be modern treasure troves.

Take for example the most basic food of all, bread. There's nothing very difficult about baking bread, yet there is a tremendous demand for good old-fashioned bread. Bread firm to the touch and fresh from the oven. All you need is flour, water, yeast and maybe an egg or two, and you're ready to start.

Perhaps you would prefer to try your hand at making ice cream or jams and marmalade using fruit fresh from organic orchards. All preserves have a ready market. So does peanut butter, crackers and cookies. All you have to do is to look for a need and supply it.

OPPORTUNITIES ARE EVERYWHERE

Four years ago, Anne A. received a cake icing set as a Christmas present from one of her young daughters. For the first few months she enjoyed experimenting and learning how to use it. Her first real test, making and icing a cake for one of her children's birthdays, was so successful that a neighbor asked Anne if she would make one for her if she supplied all the ingredients.

Again Anne's efforts were an outstanding success. News of her cake making skills spread rapidly. Twenty-five anniversary cakes and three wedding cakes later, Anne decided to give her newly found skills professional status.

Photographs and price lists of her confectionery creations were given to local wedding photographers, florists and bakeries, with an offer of 20 percent commission for every order they passed to her. She also began running a small display advertisement in the local paper.

Anne A.'s venture was successful from the word go. As the number of orders grew week by week, she was forced to employ a young woman to help her. Today, she has three bakery shops specializing entirely in cakes for special occasions and she employs a staff of 12 including the drivers for two delivery vans.

She considers that her success is based on two factors. First, only pure and organic ingredients go into her cakes; a sales point she stresses at every opportunity, especially when advertising birthday cakes for chidren. Second, every order is ready precisely when she says it will be. "I like people to know that they can rely on me," she says.

Getting Started

If kitchen products are going to be your budget builder, be prepared to start slowly as Anne did, building a clientele with neighbors and friends and gradually expanding as your experience grows. Base your prices on the cost of materials bought in small quantities and purchased as you need them. As your business grows, buying your materials in greater quantities will provide discounts and lower costs.

Packaging should be kept as inexpensive as possible. Plastic bread bags and wire ties should cost less than $5 per 1,000, while plain cake boxes will cost between 5¢ and 25¢ each depending on size.

Your success in any field will always be ensured if you have a knowledge and skill possessed by few other people. Sometimes this knowledge can be used with tremendous effect. Did you know for instance, that there is a plant growing wild in America that has built a few knowledgeable people a considerable fortune?

THE SECRET PLANT THAT'S WORTH ITS WEIGHT IN GOLD

Although there has been some controversy in several states about the claims made for ginseng, there's no doubt that it remains an extremely popular item in the natural health food stores.

Since 1714, ginseng has been hailed by some as a panacea offering stamina and long life. Others believe that the strangely shaped, licorice tasting root is the long sought elixir for good health. These claims, despite being strongly disputed by some authorities, have succeeded in creating such a desire for the plant that demand still far outstrips supply.

Ginseng is a perennial herb that is to be found growing down the length of the Appalachians and, when grown domestically, needs very little attention other than an occasional fertilizing and weeding. It is propagated by seeds and the new plants which appear in early May look something like young bean shoots.

During the second year, the bud produces two or three stems, each with up to a dozen leaflets. In the third year, a flower stem appears with small greenish flowers on tiny stalks about an inch long; the whole forming a compact cluster.

As the flowers die off, bright crimson berries form and ripen through the latter part of the year until the first frost. Each berry contains up to four seeds and it is these seeds which can be your key to early retirement.

How to Get Started

There are three ways in which you can turn ginseng into a worthwhile profit:

1. Import the dried root for sale in this country.
2. Grow the plant and sell the root by mail order or through established health food stores.
3. Sell the seeds and promote ginseng farms.

If you want to try your hand at importing and have the necessary capital, it is possible to obtain ginseng root whole or in powder form from Korea. This will give you a flying start into the ginseng business, although it will involve you in the making of overseas contacts, posting letters of credit and satisfying the restrictions on the importing of drugs into the United States.

A more casual but equally effective way of transforming ginseng into a new car or swimming pool, is by growing the plant yourself. The only drawback is that it takes a long time for your plants to reach maturity. However, if your ginseng project is combined with an intermediate venture, the long term investment will produce high profit for the small demands on your time.

Ginseng, which used to sell for 58¢ per pound, has leapt to $5 for two ounces in health food stores or a little over $30 per pound wholesale.

The area needed to grow ginseng is quite small. An area of 450 square feet will provide sufficient space for more than 1,000 plants and will earn you between $1,500 and $3,000.

The third alternative, selling the seeds, is probably the most attractive. It gives you the opportunity of getting into business much sooner. Your own farming operation begins to snowball, and it enables you to exercise your ability to build a business promoting ginseng farms along the lines of the chinchilla farms.

An outfit containing over 1,000 seeds and step-by-step instructions to grow, cultivate and market ginseng, will cost about $50. A larger outfit, with more than 3,000 ginseng seeds, sufficient to earn you up to $9,000, costs $140. The outfits may be obtained from Glass's Ginseng Exchange, Box 336, Rochdale Station, Jamaica, New York, 11434.

All of the profit building potential of ginseng applies equally to the entire family of herbs and spices.

HOW TO TURN HERBS AND SPICES INTO CASH

As with ginseng, dried herbs and spices may be bought in bulk and packaged for sale at wholesale or retail level. But in this area there is another avenue well worth exploring.

Most households have a spice rack containing an assortment of the more popular dried herbs and spices. With a little preparation you can offer the housewife an assortment of live herbs and spices growing in small pots suitable for the kitchen windowsill.

Apart from the decorative value, these small plants will provide sufficient herbs for the average household's needs. Most of the herbs are easily grown and propagated, and require little more than sufficient light and regular watering.

Your local nursery will supply you with a variety of suitable plants to get you started at a cost between 49¢ and $1 per plant. Information on the best type of soil to use and how to tend and propagate your plants may be found in almost any book on gardening.

The Markets

The housewife is the largest buyer of herbs and your method of presentation can determine your success in penetrating this market.

The best way of stimulating sales is through advertisements in newspapers or magazines. With the written word and perhaps a photograph, you can suggest the reason why people should send for your herbal plants:

"Leaves picked fresh from the plant have a better flavor than dried herbs."

"A practical and decorative asset for every kitchen."

"Surprise your friends with flavorings from your own herb garden."

THE PROFIT IN HERBS AND SPICES

Herbs and spices are easy to grow and they multiply prolifically. Half a dozen plants will provide several hundred more within a season.

Parsley, chives, sweet marjoram, sweet basil and thyme thrive in window boxes. Chervil, coriander, dill, fennel, mint, oregano, rosemary, sage and tarragon are all herbs which grow and sell easily but may be more suitable for cultivation in the garden rather than in window boxes.

There is one further possibility too important to be overlooked. With herbs, you have the unusual advantage of being able to go out into the meadows and woodlands to gather your own stock of parent plants. Most herbs gathered from the fields flourish under domestic conditions and a great many of these wild plants are unobtainable from plant nurseries.

If you are able to grow and supply herbs for culinary purposes, turning your attention to those plants which are reputed to have medicinal properties is a natural way to increase the scope of your business. There has always been considerable interest in native herbal remedies, and in this field alone you can quickly zoom to a 24-hour a day business.

HERBS AND SPICES AS MEDICINE

Herbal teas such as camomile, motherwort, rose hips, alfalfa and rosemary have a ready market. There is also an increasing public awareness of those plants which are reputed to have special curative properties; plants such as comfrey and sassafras.

Len W. had always believed that nature could ease 80 percent of human ills, but it was a magazine article dealing with the herbal plant comfrey that really intrigued him. The article stated that comfrey is not only a very fine salad green, but has been found to contain allantoin, a vital agent in the growth of new and healthy tissue. It is an easily grown, coarse-leaved plant; long famous in folk medicine.

At first, Len had no thought of making money from his convictions, but it was the difficulty he encountered while trying to buy a couple of comfrey plants that started him on his road to wealth.

No one had heard of comfrey. Len tried all the local plant nurseries and asked among friends who were gardening enthusiasts. He received many blank looks and occasionally a mention that one or two other people had been trying to buy the plant. Possibly these people had read the same article.

Then, Len eventually managed to buy three small seedlings through a mail order advertisement in a natural food magazine. Within 18 months Len W. had 200 young seedlings that he had propagated from leaves of the parent plants. Today, four years later, Len sells an average of 200 plants a week through magazine advertisements and a further 50 a week through local health stores.

Although Len is pleased at the way his business is progressing, he says that he gains the most satisfaction from the thought that he is providing the means for other people to gain what he considers to be an unusually fine natural health food.

The Markets

The sale of herbs and spices as medicine is best conducted by mail order advertisements in health food magazines or through established health food stores.

No claims should be made for specific cures unless those cures have been well substantiated. Most of the people to whom you will be selling are already well acquainted with the properties of most of the herbs you will be handling, and your advertisements can be restricted to a simple statement of what you have to offer.

Growing organic plants can lead to another big money opportunity, particularly if you have an inclination towards spare-time inventing and manufacturing.

A stroll around the garden equipment department of any large store will soon convince you of the tremendous market for gardening gadgets, especially if they can be applied to the current interest in growing organic food.

Items such as miniature greenhouses, electronic moisture controls and pH measuring instruments enjoy a steady sale. You only need one sensational, well-developed invention to take you into the millionaire class almost overnight.

For the person who is not mechanically minded, there is another area which borders on the field of organic food. It is an area which will boost your income and at the same time keep you fit enough to enjoy it.

BECOMING A DIET SPECIALIST

The man or woman who can offer sound advice on how to be healthy and beautiful has a large audience hanging on every word. If the advice is based on irrefutable fact which can be proven by specific example, the public will be willing to spend anything from a few pennies to hundreds of dollars.

The number of experts in this field is surprisingly small, and only a few of them possess doctorates or degrees in nutrition. Often, their recommendations are argumentative or contradictory, and the public swings from one widely advertised beauty or health fad to the next.

Combining organic food with sound nutrition and exercise is nothing but common sense, yet thousands of men and women are unable to arrive at this conclusion by themselves. They need someone who has been willing to study and put into practice the knowledge gained to tell them what to eat and when to eat it.

Lacking the willpower to take themselves in hand, many people will happily pay considerable sums of money to someone who will tell them exactly how to get and keep fit. They need someone to inform them which food they should eat and how much; to decide for them how many deep breaths they should take each morning and how much they should exercise every day.

These people need advice and encouragement. You can be that source of encouragement; that health and beauty advisor. How? It's as simple as preaching what you practice.

Getting Started

Read, study and learn, then put your knowledge into practice. Become a striking example of the benefits of healthy living, and turn your appearance into financial prosperity. Organize evening health classes. Offer your services as a lecturer to women's clubs. Seek recognition as a consultant to one or more of the many model or charm schools.

As your circle grows and your reputation strides ahead of you, there will be opportunities for writing regular columns in newspapers and magazines, invitations to make guest appearances on television talk shows and offers for you to endorse various commercial products for advertising purposes.

There are very few other fields where more people will be willing to listen to you and pay you well for your views, than in the field of "the lost waistlines." The fees you can demand for your services will depend on the type of groups or individuals to whom you will be speaking. Lectures to a group can vary from $20 an hour to as much as several hundred dollars, depending on your authority on the subject.

Many individuals who pay $10 or $20 a week to visit a health spa would be more than willing to pay the same amount to attend your classes; especially if friends had convinced them that you produce results.

It is only a short step from good health and vitality to vitamins, and although vitamins may not be considered food in the strict sense of the word, they certainly have an organic aspect and profit potential which makes them well worth considering.

HUGE PROFITS FROM VITAMINS

Any product which has as widespread consumer acceptance as vitamins is always worth investigating. Where there is a large and steady demand for a product, somewhere nearby is an opportunity for the spare-time businessman to reach out for wealth.

When manufacturers and retailers are able to offer $10 bottles of vitamins on a 1¢ sale, vitamins have to be a high profit business. It is a business which can be adapted to individualized operation in two ways.

How to Get Started

With a modest investment you may buy brand-name vitamins from a wholesaler and resell them. There are, of course, several brands which will not be available to you, but there are many others from which to choose. Give yourself a marketing advantage by refusing the chemically compounded vitamins and insisting on vitamins derived from an organic source.

You will find that the wholesale prices of vitamins will allow you considerable profit. For example:

For a slightly larger investment, many of the major manufacturers of vitamins will supply tablets in bulk for local packaging under your own name. A quantity of 50,000 Vitamin C tablets will cost about $100 and other tablets have a similar discount.

Bulk buying will involve you in the purchase of printed labels and cartons or bottles for packaging. These may be obtained in quantities to suit your budget. Usually, the larger the order, the smaller the unit cost. Plastic bottles suitable for 100 tablets cost approximately 4¢ each with cap. Bottles for 500 tablets cost a trifle more at 7¢ each.

Adhesive labels from your local printer will cost about $15 per 5,000 for the first run. Subsequent printings will be slightly cheaper.

The Markets

The first customers of most spare-time businesses are friends, neighbors and work colleagues. As you expand, you may want to consider setting up a stall in an outdoor farmer's market or setting out to organize sales through house-to-house vitamin parties.

If you should decide that there is greater potential in bulk packaging and wholesaling, your markets will be local stores and supermarkets. Most of the larger chain stores have a central buying office, and successful application to the head buyer with an agreement for deliveries to be made to the main warehouse could prove very time saving.

You should also consider advertising in health food magazines such as **Prevention**; offering your packaged vitamins at a price competitive to similar products in the magazine. Further sales may be achieved by advertising in magazines which specialize in offering merchandise to people who are interested in business opportunities.

With vitamins, as with every other product to which the term organic can be applied, your sales will skyrocket as you stress the health-giving properties of natural foods. Take a vital interest in the well-being of your customers and your first million is as inevitable as blossoms in springtime.

Chapter 10

How to Make Money in the Big Interest Field Of Fishing

Now we get to one of the really big categories, if not the very biggest. Photography runs a close second, but fishing probably attracts more enthusiasts than any other recreational activity.

By now the pattern has become clear. Without a doubt you can make immense sums of money in your spare time. Opportunities surround you, and when there is widespread interest in any type of activity, the opportunites in that field are simply begging for someone to come along and reap a golden harvest. Are you that someone? What better field could there be than fishing?

Almost without effort you can divide the opportunites to make money in fishing into several different steps. All of them rich with potential, and all of them within your reach.

Providing products is the first general step, and this can be divided into countless smaller steps, any one of which can be your way to wealth.

PROVIDING PRODUCTS THAT ANGLERS NEED

At first, it would appear that an angler's needs are few—a fishing rod, a line and reel, a hook and some bait. A closer look, however, will quickly show that there is far more involved than those simple pieces of equipment.

Fishing or angling has kept pace with the times. If Izaak Walton could take a look into the tackle box of a modern fisherman, he would be amazed. Nylon line, plastic floats, artificial lures and electronic sensors. Today's fishermen have been aided by, or are the victims of, science, technology and commercialism. Undoubtedly, the opportunities to make money are enormous.

How to Get Started

If you find it difficult to walk along the banks of a stream without feeling a tremendous urge to bait up and cast a line into the water, you're already hooked. You are what is known as an "enthusiastic fisherman," and as such you are already well aware of items that are needed or equipment that could be improved upon.

For you, the steps ahead lead directly to the big money. You need no other guidance, just a few words of encouragement. For heaven's sake, go ahead, get started. Produce those items, make those improvements—but do it now.

For those whose enthusiasm has yet to be awakened or are overwhelmed by mass production and coast-to-coast advertising, take heart. The opportunities are still there, you'll just have to work a little harder, that's all.

This isn't a full list, there are hundreds more products used by fishermen. If one of them lights a fire of inspiration within you, that first step has already been taken. If none of them appeal to you, keep looking. There's going to be at least one which strikes a spark.

Floats, plugs, minnow traps, reels, rods, keep nets, keep lines, disgorgers, bait boxes, weights, hook boxes, creels, line dressing, reel maintenance kits, scaling knives, artificial bait, live bait, rod rests, spring balances, wire traces, bite alarms, thermometers, landing nets, spoons and spinners, comprise only a partial list. You can take any one of those items and divide it up even more.

For example, rods come in many types. If you were contemplating making fishing rods in your spare time—"Custom-made, perfectly balanced. Good to look at, a joy to handle and designed to catch fish."—you would have to consider if they would be wooden, metal, fiberglass, hollow, solid, one piece, several pieces, expandable, long, short, fresh water, shore casting, deep sea, spinning, or fly rods.

Any one of these could be your own, individual, specialized field. All you have to do is visualize a specific need and then set out to satisfy it.

Marketing is no problem. There are hundreds of sporting goods stores which will be very happy to handle a new product, especially if you can demonstrate the need for it. There is also a great number of magazines and newspapers which would be ideal media for mail order advertising.

Joe L. lived close to the River Avon. A swift flowing river that courses through the green English countryside—a fisherman's paradise. It seemed to Joe that the most successful bait was bread crust or a dough made with flour and water, sometimes with a little cheese added. The trouble was that the bait refused to stay on the hook for very long in that swift flowing water.

He gave the problem considerable thought for a while, read some books, asked a manufacturer to send some samples and within a year, Joe was in the bait manufacturing business.

Joe's idea was to add chewing gum to the bread dough. Through reading, he discovered the ingredient used in the manufacture of chewing gum and wrote to one of the importers who handled this special product; a form of base gum. The importer sent him three pieces of this rock-like substance.

By experimenting, heating it and adding oils, glycerine and thinning agents, Joe discovered how to keep the gum soft and pliable while retaining its tenacity in water.

It proved a deadly bait, soon to be copied by bigger industrial bait manufacturers. But by that time, Joe had made more than $500,000 and was already branching out into the manufacture of automatic depth-adjusting floats.

One of the secrets of Joe's success was that his advertising stressed big catches of big fish.

THERE'S BIG MONEY IN THE BIG ONES

Any experienced fisherman will tell you that there can be as much pleasure in landing some of the smaller, more cautious and harder fighting fish, as there is in going after the big ones. But when it comes to anything to do with catching fish, the stress has to be on hooking the big ones. The big one that got away is a phrase in every fisherman's vocabulary. If you are lacking big money ideas, begin slanting your thinking toward those monsters that lurk in the older lakes and rivers.

Let's go back to that thought about the big one, but one that didn't get away. Let's imagine that you or someone you know, has landed one of these monsters. Try to figure ways in which that spectacular catch can be turned into cash.

First, who would be interested? Naturally, the person who lands this big fish is interested. But there are others who would be interested; people who would be prepared to pay cash. There is only one thing they require—proof. Either in photographs or the fish itself.

Who are these people and why do they want proof? They are the manufacturers of the hook which caught the fish, the line that was used, the rod, the reel, the boat, the outboard motor, the lure and the landing net that brought that big fish into the boat.

And it doesn't end there. If that fish was caught at a private sporting lake, the owner of that property would be able to use photographs of such a catch in advertising brochures. Chambers of Commerce and travel bureaus also need such pictures, and so do land development companies who are building lakeside or riverside housing developments near where the catch was made.

Here is a sneaky little bit of information worth putting in your tackle box. If it is your fish or you are on hand when it is caught, assuming you can be sufficiently persuasive, arrange to have the fish stuffed as quickly as possible.

A manufacturer may be prepared to pay big money for pictures of the fish being caught, but given the choice he would prefer to be on hand personally. He would be accompanied by a camera crew using specialized photographic equipment and a representative from his advertising agency, complete with layout sketch and foreknowledge of exactly the type of picture required.

It's very difficult to tell from a photograph whether the fish being pulled from the water or dangling from the end of a line is live and wriggling or simply stuffed. The event was true, the fish real, the only thing different is the time the catch took place.

Big fish, thinking big—they are almost the same thing, especially if you would like to make fishing your way of life when you retire.

HOW TO RETIRE WITH A FISH FARM

Jeff P. was almost due to retire. He found himself a small piece of land close by a river and bought himself a house. From then on, Saturdays and Sundays were a fisherman's dream of heaven. His wife was content and his three sons would often bring their families to visit and enjoy excellent fishing.

Gradually, almost imperceptibly, the area became more popular and fishing clubs chartered buses to take them to the attractive parts of the river. It was these clubs, together with Jeff's skill that showed him the steps to more money than he had ever imagined possible.

The river was beautiful, sided by banks made for picnics; but it was a deceptive river. The clear, swiftly flowing water housed handsome trout and giant catfish. There were bass and carp, and bluegills abounded in the shallow parts.

But there they stayed. Only the luckiest or the most skillful fisherman enjoyed the triumph of fish for supper. All except Jeff. There he sat, always in the same spot, pulling fish out of the river with almost monotonous regularity. Quite often he would give some of his catch to families fishing near him. He was a happy man and he enjoyed his fishing.

He became a "local character." A character with the reputation of being a master fisherman. Visitors and members of fishing clubs began to offer to buy his catch rather than return home empty-handed. This demand became so great on weekends, that Jeff began keeping the fish he caught during the week in a small lake he dug on his property.

Eventually, Jeff bought more land and built three large trout pools, and began advertising his fishing facilities. He arranged with a trout hatchery to supply him with young trout at between 15¢ and 25¢ per pound. As the young fish gained weight in his pools, Jeff was able to charge $1.25 a pound for fish caught by visitors to the ponds.

Today, Jeff and his sons own 15 trout farms in different parts of the country. But Jeff has only just revealed the secret of his ability to catch fish in that difficult to fish river.

It seems that every morning he would grind up scraps of food and throw them into the river, always at the same spot. It became a feeding place for the fish and Jeff always made certain that he was secure in his spot before the weekend visitors began arriving.

With knowledge of fishing, spare time and a desire to make money, Jeff was soon earning more money in a month than he had been able to earn in six months at his full-time employment.

Fishing lends itself so well to other spare-time hobbies, that moneymaking is almost inevitable. Electronics is a very good example of a hobby that combines very well with fishing.

ELECTRONIC GADGETS FOR THE ANGLER

Electronic technology has already made itself felt in the field of fishing. There are electronic scanners which will tell you how deep the water is, whether fish are present and the precise temperature at any depth. There are electronic devices which will warn you when you have a bite and there are even lures which will send out vibrations that attract fish. Jerry W. is presently working on a way to send electrical impulses into the ground to force worms to come to the surface.

The field of electronics is advancing with such speed that it would be impossible to suggest new devices. The equipment and gadgets which will be in everyday use only a year from now, have not been invented yet. The field is becoming so technically involved it is impossible to even visualize new inventions. But if you have a background in electronics and a fertile mind, you will already be putting your mind to work on new possibilities.

Marketing your ideas will not be difficult. The demand for new gadgets has been at a high level for many years and will continue to grow for many more. It is an enormously hungry market.

The three most effective methods of marketing would be:

1. Mail order, with advertisements in fishing magazines and Sunday newspaper supplements.
2. Directly to the retailer by advertisements in sporting goods magazines.
3. Through sports goods wholesalers.

Your profit margin can only be determined after the cost factor has been established. If there are similar products already on the market, you will be able to arrive at an approximate retail price. But it is obvious that without knowledge of the product, it is impossible to give any guidance on prices.

Meeting a demand will always ensure sales, especially when the price is attractive. As mentioned earlier, it is sometimes possible to combine two or more different ventures and produce an item with tremendous moneymaking possibilities.

A PUBLICATION THAT ANGLERS WILL WANT TO BUY

Here is a product which combines fishing and publishing. It is a publication which is aimed directly at the fisherman, but adds the high moneymaking potential of small-time publishing. The publication is a guide to fishing waters and, if pursued correctly, can be one of the greatest moneymaking ventures you could ever undertake. Try these steps and find out what it feels like to be wealthy.

How to Get Started

First, imagine the publication as you, an ardent fisherman, would like to receive it. It should fit within a certain framework and contain specific information. Let's take a look at this publication, this high demand item, which could be your stairway to the world of immense riches.

1. It must be easily affordable, say, $2 to $5.
2. It must be a convenient size, perhaps paperback size, with maybe 24 to 48 pages.
3. It should confine itself to specific areas. In this way a series of booklets can be produced, each of them providing information on areas which are readily accessible.
4. It must be regularly brought up-to-date so that the information is always reliable.

Now let's take a closer look at the possibilities and determine some of the ways of establishing such a publication. The possibilities are self-evident. The demand for an information-filled booklet enabling the fisherman to get the most from his hobby would be enormous.

The booklet should contain in-depth information on fishing waters within boundaries determined by the location. For instance, in Oregon where fishing waters are plentiful, the booklet would cover relatively small areas, giving information on perhaps 20 or 30 rivers, lakes and streams. But in parts of southern California where fishing facilities are scarce, the booklet would have to cover a much larger area to provide even a dozen fishing locations.

The information provided by the booklet would consist of details on the species of fish to be caught, suggestions on how to catch those fish (bait, hooks, time of day, etc.) and maps showing exactly how to get to the fishing spots.

As the booklets develop, they could be illustrated with photographs taken at the various fishing sites and, to whet the appetites of prospective buyers of the booklets, photographs of fish being caught.

It is obvious that you cannot sit down and produce a series of such booklets in one evening. To produce even one issue is going to take considerable knowledge and research, but each succeeding publication will get easier.

Now we get down to details. The where, the how and the who. First, where do you get the necessary information? Well, preferably first hand. Start locally, or in an area with which you are well acquainted and, best of all, where you personally have fished.

If you haven't fished these waters yourself, try to get authentic information from someone who has. Failing in this, talk to local inhabitants and park rangers. The local chamber of commerce may be able to help and of course there is always that fountain of information, the public library. Always try to ensure that the information you obtain is accurate.

Next is the how. Producing a book of this nature is really very easy. When you have assembled a fair amount of information and are in a position of being able to gauge the final length and size of the book, talk to a local printer and let him give you some ideas on production.

Better still, talk to several printers and get lots of ideas. It won't cost you anything to talk to them and you will undoubtedly discover that some printers will be more imaginative than others. Most importantly, some will quote better prices than others.

Finally, there is the who. Who will sell your book? We already know who will buy them, and knowing who will buy them, we know who is going to sell them. You are going to sell them, and any store that sells fishing tackle is going to sell them.

Your selling will be through advertisements in local newspapers. When you have covered a large part of the country, it will be worth advertising in a national magazine. But while you are still building, national advertising would be unprofitable. Very few fisherman living in Boston or Idaho are going to be interested in the streams of your distant locality.

Now we reach the subject which is of paramount importance—profit. What sort of returns can you expect?

Eventually, your profits will be enormous. As with most spare-time ventures, however, you have to lift it off the ground gently, steadily and with applied effort.

The more booklets you have printed, the lower the unit cost. The printer will be able to advise you on the most economical way to get started. Later, as your sales build and you begin preparing the second booklet in the series, you will have a better insight as to the most economical way to proceed.

Before leaving this subject, there is a final point which must not be overlooked. It is possibly the most important point of all and it could build your profits beyond anything you are dreaming about at this moment.

Every booklet should be crammed with advertisements. Local tackle stores, equipment manufacturers, campgrounds, restaurants, car rentals and private airfields are all potential advertisers and it is from them that your greatest profit can be derived.

To persuade such people to advertise, ask your printer to prepare you a dummy booklet, similar to the one you will be publishing. Allocate spaces for advertisements and then specify advertising rates for a quarter page, half page and full page.

Show this dummy booklet to the people you would like to include in your publication and tell them all about the booklet—who will read it and how it will help this business-man increase his business.

When he agrees to run an advertisement in your booklet, sign him to a contract, calling for him to pay on publication. Don't be afraid to ask for a signature on a contract. Businessmen are used to being asked to sign such contracts. It is not that you don't trust him, it is simply the correct way to conduct this type of business.

Almost any aspect of fishing can be turned into profit. All you have to do is think like a fisherman. And what can be more frustrating to an enthusiastic fisherman than to be out on a trip, unexpectedly run across an ideal fishing spot and then remember that he has left his fishing equipment at home?

THE BOAT, ROD AND REEL RENTAL BUSINESS

Even the rental business will provide at least three steps to making money in your spare time. The first step is very obvious. You rent a site at a lake, beside a river or near any popular fishing resort. You prepare yourself with a stock of fishing tackle and equipment and you proceed to rent it to visitors.

You ask for a returnable deposit equal to the value of the equipment you are leasing. When it is brought back, you return the deposit, less your charges for rental.

That's the first way to make money in the rental business. Of course, there's a little more to it than that, but there's no tricks or catches. A little thought, a small investment in used rods and reels, and you're on your way.

The same methods of business apply to boat rentals, but naturally, you are faced with a bigger investment. The boat, rod and reel rental business does, however, present an ideal weekend spare-time venture.

A run-off venture from the rental business is that of repairs to the rental equipment. This does not offer too great a proposition, although it can be a steady source of income, easily tied into a complimentary venture. Rental equipment is subject to a great deal of hard use and repairs are usually part of the overhead. But as mentioned, it is primarily a weekend business and the part-time businessman will usually do the repairs and overhauls to equipment himself during the week.

The third way of making money in the rental business is by selling equipment to the people who do the renting. Robert V. started his selling casually, but with the thoughtful intention of developing his spare-time venture into an above average income.

He began by contacting manufacturers of boats and fishing equipment. Some he contacted by letter, others he contacted personally. The responses he obtained were very encouraging and, with gentle guidance, his business began growing.

Robert was very fortunate in that he owned a van and he spent several days fitting it out as a traveling showroom. When it was completed he had a representative stock of rods, reels and tackle from most of the leading manufacturers. Some items he had bought at wholesale prices, but most had been given him as samples. The manufacturers thought that his ideas and drive were worth supporting.

Leaving Friday, after finishing his regular job as a factory storekeeper, Robert spent the weekend visiting recreational areas. He spoke to owners of rental equipment and encouraged them to expand their business by purchasing the latest equipment.

Not only did Robert offer rods, reels and tackle, but he also sold clothing, books, spare parts and outboard motors. Strapped to the top of his van were four fiberglass kayaks and an inflatable rowboat.

His business has now reached $3,000 a month, a stage where he will be able to take a three week vacation and tour the recreational areas which are too distant for him to reach on a weekend.

His customers look forward to his regular visits and usually have orders waiting for him, but the orders he receives by mail are sufficient to keep him busy every minute of his spare time.

One of the secrets of Robert's success is his thorough knowledge of the products he sells. This product knowledge is essential in every form of selling. It can also be the means of establishing a different type of spare-time income.

HOW TO SELL YOUR FISHING SKILLS

The most skillful fisherman will be interested in anything which will enable him to be even more skillful. The man or woman who wins all the fishing contests will always be interested in anything which will provide even bigger catches. The novice will want to know about anything which will turn him or her into a near expert.

The thirst for knowledge is insatiable. If this were not true, there would be fewer libraries, schools, colleges and universities. Newspapers would not exist and instructors in every field would be looking for work. If you have knowledge of any kind you can sell it, and this is true of fishing.

Perhaps you've never won a fishing contest. Perhaps you've never held the world's record for landing a super fish and maybe you've never invented a new gadget to make fishing easier or more certain. But if you are an enthusiast of the leisurely art of fishing, you have knowledge that someone will buy.

How to Get Started

First, take a good look at your interest in fishing. What aspect of it interests you most? Which fish do you prefer to catch? Why? What bait do you use? Where do you fish? Exactly how do you fish? When do you fish?

Now, perhaps for the first time, you've discovered that you have definite preferences. Perhaps you prefer fishing from a boat rather than from the bank of a stream. Maybe you like working with a plug or a spinner, or it could be that your technique with an artificial worm always gets results.

Whatever your preferences, whatever your skills and techniques, these factors comprise your knowledge. This is what experience has taught you—and you can sell it.

Almost every magazine which has articles on fishing will pay well for useful hints and tips. These pieces may be short, perhaps between 100 to 500 words, and sometimes illustrated with a sketch or photographs. Payment can range from $25 to $250, depending on the magazine and the length of the contribution. A more ambitious effort, perhaps a full length article, 5,000 or so words long, will bring correspondingly higher payment.

If you doubt your ability to write a few sentences, let alone an article for a magazine, give it a try. Start out on the hints and tips and write as if you were telling a friend. You'll find it's easier than you think.

After the first two or three tips are published, you'll suddenly discover you like writing these conversational pieces. You'll find too, that you'll like the checks which arrive in the mail.

However, this is only a step. As your writing skill increases you'll find that there are opportunities to write regular columns; not only for those magazines which are directed at the fisherman, but for all the newspapers and magazines which mention outdoor activities.

If your ability to write is really zero and not just a doubt, you can still sell your knowledge. All you need is a friend who is willing to do the writing for you in return for a share of the income.

Taken a step further, there is no reason why the same methods should not be applied to the writing of a series of booklets or even a full length book. Knowledge is worth hard cash. Make it work for you.

There would be very few fish caught if there were no such thing as bait. A pointed stick may be very effective in the hands of an Eskimo or New Guinea hunter, but without bait most of us would give up fishing altogether. So, we have a product in high demand and we have a very large number of customers—why are we waiting?

THE HIGHLY PROFITABLE BAIT
BUSINESS

The first step is to determine exactly what you know about bait, and it is a subject which is more complex than you might at first suppose. However, it is big business.

How to Get Started

There is really only one way to make big money in the bait business and that is to grow the bait and sell it. It's possible that instead of growing the bait (live bait), you may prefer to manufacture it.

Under this second heading would come such baits as cheese, cheese dough, marshmallows, bread doughs, hemp seeds and obscure mixtures which contain special additives such as oil of aniseed, fish oils and so on.

While it is quite likely that you could get into the bait manufacturing business and make a lot of money (many people do), the highest profit comes from the live bait business.

If you are not already aware of the fact, you should know that there is a very large number of different types of bait; all of which you can grow and all of which are in very great demand. Let's take a look at some of them.

- Worms. The universal bait and the biggest money spinner of them all. We will go further into this in a moment.

- Hellgrammite

- Gall worms

- Catalpa worms

- Caddis worms

- Meal worms

- Maggots

- Grasshoppers and crickets

All of these are natural baits and most of them can be grown in sufficient quantities to provide a very substantial income.

In Europe, where maggots are a more popular bait, a considerable number of enterprising men and women have climbed to a six figure income by encouraging the breeding habits of flies; in particular the Calliphora Erythrocephala, the blue-bottle fly.

Reg M. started in a small way, working evenings and weekends. He would breed his maggots in a cellar of his house. With experience, he learned how to time their growth so that on Friday evening and Saturday morning he could deliver a gallon of fresh and wriggling maggots to each of his customers.

His customers were a fast-growing number of fishing tackle stores. They paid Reg $5 a gallon for his maggots and resold them at 50¢ a scoop to weekend anglers. There were about 25 scoops in each gallon, so the retailer showed a fair profit for his investment.

Reg was assured of a steady demand because the retailer had to throw away any unsold maggots by Sunday, since by that time they were beginning to turn into larvae and, by Tuesday or Wednesday, into flies.

Today, Reg has three large greenhouses which are in fact maggot factories. His spare-time venture has become a full-time big business, bringing him more than $80,000 a year.

Under carefully controlled conditions, Reg exposes horse meat for the attention of the flies, and the resulting maggots are sorted for size on grading machines which Reg designed.

The maggots are cleaned in a bed of bran. Some are colored by being immersed in flourescent dyes and they are then packaged in insulated containers and delivered by express all over the country.

Reg saw an opportunity for making money and pursued it to the limit. What he can do, you can do. The bait market is still virtually untouched, except perhaps for the worm business.

The worm business became over-commercialized. So many people were convinced that there was money to be made growing worms, that they were prepared to pay large sums of money to buy a bed of worms and a book of instructions.

Almost unnoticeably, the market changed. Instead of the larger growers selling their worms to the tackle shops with all that it entailed—packaging, delivering, invoicing, etc.— they began concentrating on selling to people who wanted to be growers.

To induce sales in a market that got very competitive, they told prospective growers that there was such a demand for worms they would buy back at cost price all the worms that the growers could supply.

In no time at all, these new growers were looking around for other people who wanted to be growers, and then selling them a bed of worms and breeding instructions for $500 or $600. The original market, the fisherman, was almost completely neglected.

If you want to get into the worm business, do it now. There's a lot of money in those wriggly creatures, even if you are only selling to anglers. You can buy your first batch of worms from a commercial grower (they advertise in fishing magazines) or you can simply start with a handful of worms from your own garden.

Before leaving the subject of bait, there are three other creatures which fish consider good food. They are crawfish, frogs and waterdogs. These three baits are very expensive, and the reason is that few people have discovered how to breed them commercially. So just there, in that small group of baits, could be your spare-time steps to a fortune. Tied in with these live baits is the opportunity to specialize in a way which can build a regular income.

A SPECIAL LIVE BAIT SERVICE

Fisherman who like to use live bait have one common complaint. They object to the fact that much of the live bait they purchase is not as live as it should be. The carton of worms they bought earlier that morning was found to contain more than a third of dead worms, while the remainder were limp and sluggish. Hardly the bait to tempt a cautious fish.

Perhaps the store from which the worms had been bought was too warm. Perhaps the carton had been on the shelf for two or three weeks. Whatever the reason, many anglers are inclined to be disappointed in the quality of the live bait they buy. Their special needs are your opportunities.

How to Get Started

The first requirement, the very essence of this business, is a steady supply of live bait that is really "live". Whether you grow it or breed it yourself, or whether you know where you can obtain a steady supply from the fields and lakes, is unimportant. The essential facts are that the bait must be fresh and there must be a continuous supply.

Once you have your supply of live bait secured, the marketing is not difficult but it does require thought and planning. Your methods of selling will be determined to a large extent by the type of bait you are going to sell.

Insects such as worms, grasshoppers and meal worms require little more than controlled temperature and moisture. Waterdogs on the other hand would require tanks of water continuously aerated.

Your main objective is to get to the angler directly and this can be achieved in several ways:

1. By touring popular fishing spots at rivers, streams and lakes, and selling to the weekend anglers. This can be accomplished in a van specially fitted to transport the type of bait you are going to sell. These tours must be regular so that anglers will get to rely on you being there week after week.

2. By advertising "Live Bait For Sale" in your local newspaper.

3. By circulating in local fishing clubs, a flyer advertising your live bait.

4. By establishing a small bait and tackle shack close to a well-frequented fishing spot.

The amount of money you make can be considerable. John F., who tours a midwest river every weekend in a well-equipped truck, estimates making four times as much money in the two days at the river, than he does working as a janitor in a hospital the other five days of the week.

John sells live bait and manufactured bait, and then adds to his profit with a good selection of hooks, weights, lines, floats and most of the fishing equipment that anglers can be tempted to buy; especially if they are having a poor day and consider that a change of tactics will change their luck.

From fishing to photography is an easy step. A tremendous number of people enjoy both pastimes. Perhaps the relaxation of fishing provides the peace of mind which encourages creativity. It could be that the tranquility of a river bank or forgotten lake is aesthetically satisfying. Whatever the reason, making money in one field is as easy as making it in the other.

Chapter 11

How to Make Money in the Big Interest Field of Photography

As with fishing, photography has its devotees and to an even greater extent, photography has its range of equipment and accessories. Most importantly, however, photography has branches which spread into every corner of modern day living.

Apart from its position as a very popular hobby, photography has applications in all types of manufacturing. It is used in the selling of almost every product on the market, it is used in the construction of skyscrapers and it is taken underground on mining projects. Photography is an important part of medicine, is used extensively as a teaching aid and is an essential part of space exploration.

With a subject so vast and complex, it would be impossible to mention even a small part of its moneymaking possibilities. For that, you will have to set your own mind to work. To give it a little encouragement, let's take a look at one or two of the less obvious ways to make money in photography.

HOW TO MAKE RETOUCHING PAY

To the uninitiated, photo retouching sounds like a highly skilled, very exclusive profession—one that requires years of training. It is skilled and it is an exclusive profession, but only because so few venture into it. Sometimes the years of training are necessary, but very rarely. What is more important is the desire to work in the art field. Anyone who cannot pick up the elementary basic skills of photo retouching in a few weeks, will never develop the skills which can only come with experience.

How to Get Started

1. Buy a set of retouching brushes and two or three retouching dyes from your local photo supplies store. Use black and grey dyes to start with, then color as experience grows.

2. Buy or borrow a book which tells you how to apply those dyes in photo coloring and photo retouching.

With the growth of color photography, coloring prints by hand has become a lost art, but the skills still apply to photo retouching.

3. Find some old black and white prints to experiment with.

Janet M. had left college with the intention of becoming a professional artist, but it wasn't long before she realized that her ability to visualize and produce pictures commercially were way below what she would need to provide herself with a living wage.

She found it easier to photograph scenes, project them onto a canvas, outline them with a pencil and then apply the colors. But it took her so long to produce the paintings and sell them that she became totally discouraged.

Janet took a job as a receptionist in a commercial photography studio and soon discovered that many of the prints and transparencies taken by the photographers were sent out to a professional retoucher.

This retoucher would remove power lines from pictures, put a sheen on metal products and remove unwanted reflections, cover small flaws caused during processing and generally improve the quality of the finished work.

Before long, Janet had learned some of the techniques of retouching and airbrushing. She took home a pile of discarded prints and transparencies and started to become proficient in the art of retouching.

Janet still works as a receptionist in the commercial photography studio. She likes the work and it keeps her in touch with people in the profession. But in her spare time she does photo retouching with a skill to match the high degree of professionalism required. Her work as a receptionist pays her $5 an hour, but she gets $30 an hour for her retouching skills, and special jobs bring her more than twice that amount.

Photo retouching is for the person interested in art, the person with patience and the person willing to learn. It is an extremely high-paying profession and one in which anyone can become involved.

OPPORTUNITIES FOR MICROFILMING

Almost every home in the country is the target for a deluge of printed material. From the daily newspaper, the **T.V. Guide**, monthly magazines and supermarket flyers, to the once a year Internal Revenue forms—there is non-stop flow of reading matter.

To people in business, that flow is a thundering avalanche; a continuous barrage of printed paper that has to be read. Sometimes not only read but committed to memory and then filed for future reference. Added to this relentless pressure of material received through the mail is the printed material generated by the business itself. Invoices, statements, bills of lading, costings, sales reports, sales brochures and advertising layouts are typical examples.

It has been calculated that the printed material which passes through a medium-sized business in 12 months would, if kept, completely fill a three-bedroom house from ground floor to attic. A great deal of this material, destroyed in self-defense, should be filed for future reference.

Very little else need be said. Microfilming machines are not inexpensive, nor are they beyond the reach of anyone who can afford a small automobile.

For the person with initiative, the way is wide open. A microfilming machine, a foolproof filing system and personal application to progressive businesses, combined with a guarantee of honor, security, confidentiality and reliability— make a continually mounting income inevitable. If you have the drive to succeed, no further words should be necessary. The opportunity has been revealed, how you handle it is up to you.

The reverse is true with regard to real estate photography. Here, the opportunity is obvious. How to approach it as a spare-time business may need a little explanation.

SELLING A SPECIALIZED SERVICE TO REALTORS

Realtors have been using photographs to sell property for many years. The concept of taking photographs of the exterior of a house and showing that photograph to prospective clients has not changed a great deal since the idea first became popular.

If you can take attractive pictures and are prepared to do a little hard selling, it is possible to introduce new trends into the real estate business—trends which can bring you a large second income.

The photography in this venture is really secondary. The pictures have to be good and they have to be pictures which sell the product—in this instance, a house or property. No doubt, as the venture picks up speed, the photographs will alter in character; emphasizing features which are found to be important, and playing down features which would be detrimental to a sale.

But the primary thrust of this venture is a selling job. You have to make personal contact with the heads of the more progressive real estate companies and you have to sell them on your idea.

How to Get Started

Begin by explaining to the real estate director something he already knows. "When someone wants to buy a house they come to you, and after you have ascertained area, type of house and price, that person is taken by car to visit several houses that are on your listings. This time-consuming procedure is acted out time after time until the customer is satisfied and a sale is made."

The realtor will usually agree and you can now tell him how he can save a great deal of time—both his own and his prospective customer's—and, at the same time increase his percentage of sales.

Your task is to sell the realtor on the idea of setting up a comfortable room with armchairs, a coffee table with coffee served in china cups, a 35mm. slide projector, screen and a transparency file containing well-photographed slides of all the current listings. The slides would be arranged and cross-indexed to provide ready availability to pictures of property by area and by price.

Your selling point would be that by seating the prospective buyers in comfortable surroundings, they can be shown a vast selection of houses or other types of property in a fraction of the time that it would take to visit them physically. Not only is there a saving in time, but in the congenial surroundings of a comfortable lounge it is much easier for the salesperson to explain the selling points of the property.

Another point worth stressing is that the photographs can be taken under ideal conditions and at the seller's convenience. This would also include photography of the interior; an advantage not enjoyed by the salesperson who has to fit viewing times to the mutual convenience of both seller and buyer—a feat which often proves difficult.

Your profit? A contract to take all the photographs for the next 12 months or more, at a fee of $25 to $250 per house, depending on the type of house and the number of pictures required.

It is possible under some circumstances to arrange to sell the projector and screen to the realtor and make additional profit. However this is a minor source of income compared with your income from the photography.

The type of photography that is used for interior decoration in homes, restaurants and many places of business can be considered a spare-time venture sufficiently important to be tackled exclusively, or it could be part of the real estate venture. After all, your exposure to many different styles of homes and businesses will give you a very good insight as to the type of art that is selling.

PHOTOGRAPHY IN INTERIOR DECORATION

The type of photographs you like to take are your own individual interpretation of the world around you. Any one of the millions of subjects can be interpreted in many ways, flavored by your opinions and your taste.

Take the nude, for example. Here we have a subject that has been used in art from the time sketching began. Photographs and paintings of the nude can be found in many homes and businesses today; most of these pictures being both tasteful and decorative.

But as a photographer you would know that the nude can be presented in a multitude of ways. Black and white, color, silhouette, high key, solarized, montage and reversal are just a few of these ways.

This great range of technique can be applied to any subject, and your own personal expression of what you want to illustrate enables you to offer the public interior decor they can obtain nowhere else. Turn this important fact to your advantage.

How to Get Started

If making money in photography is a project which interests you, we must assume you either know how to take presentable pictures or are willing to learn. We must also assume you have the necessary equipment or at least a camera. The processing can be done through a trade processing house.

We now have four steps. First, you must take the pictures. Second, you must have them processed in the way you have previsualized and in the size required. Third, you must mount and frame them in a way which makes them both attractive and acceptable to the market at which you are aiming. Fourth, you have to sell these works of art.

The first three steps are directed entirely by your personal preferences. This is what gives them that unmistakable stamp of individuality. The fourth step, the selling, is a mechanical business arrangement which you can either leave to someone else to handle for you or, preferably, accept it as part of the business in which you are engaged.

Don't feel that because you are an "artist" you want no part of that vulgar subject called commerce. You and I both know that you are in this to make money, so make as much as you can.

If you can thoroughly enjoy the way in which you make money, so much the better. That's how it should be.

Following are the ways in which you can sell your pictures. The prices you ask will depend on the size of your reputation and the going price for original works of art.

1. Directly to the customer by:
   (a) Exhibitions at fairs and art displays.
   (b) Direct mail, using an illustrated brochure.
   (c) By advertising both locally and in the Sunday supplements.
2. By placing them in an art dealer's showroom and arranging for them to be sold on commission.
3. By working through a salesman whose job it is to call on art dealers.

Sometimes a restaurant owner will let you place a selection of your pictures on the walls of his restaurant. In the corner of each picture would be your business card and the price of the picture. This provides the restaurateur with a continually changing interior decor and, if you agree, a percentage of the sales on all pictures.

If you are well into photography, you will already be aware of the special decorative materials on which photographs can be printed. Linens, plastics, wood and textured film are a few of the interesting surfaces which can be used for photographic interior decor. There are so many ways to make money in your spare time with photography and making photographic copies of old pictures is one of those ways. It could be a venture you would like to pursue.

A SPECIALIZED COPY SERVICE

At first thought it would appear that there is insufficient demand for copies of old pictures to provide even a modest income. This may be true of the general run of copy work, but there is an area which is virtually untouched and it may be one which interests you.

When you think of photographic copies, you think about people who find pictures in an album or tucked away in a drawer. They would like another copy of this picture for one reason or another, but they have lost the negative. Consequently, the picture has to be photographed and another negative made.

As you can imagine, these circumstances do not occur often enough to warrant the purchase of special equipment or even to make advertising for such work a very lucrative proposition. There is an opening, however.

How to Get Started

First, ask yourself what type of pictures are likely to lack negatives. Perhaps the negatives have been lost or are now unobtainable. The answer lies in old family pictures—pictures of grandparents and great-grandparents.

Now that we know the type of pictures, we have to ask ourselves who would want copies of these pictures and why. The answer to this question is people interested in genealogy. Genealogy is becoming increasingly popular. More and more people are becoming interested in tracing their ancestors. Several religions, especially the Church of Jesus Christ of Latter-day Saints or the Mormons, have a deep-rooted interest in genealogy.

A specialized service to genealogical associations and other groups with similar interests will bring you as much photographic copy work as you can handle. An advertisement placed where it can be seen by people interested in ancestral research will quickly build you a specialized service copying old photographs.

Specialization in photography can be a profitable avenue, especially if you can select areas which are not already saturated. Portraiture, weddings and school photography

are so crammed with photographers that making progress in
these fields would be relatively slow. Fortunately, there are
other areas not quite so crowded.

HORTICULTURAL PHOTOGRAPHY

Can you photograph flowers and trees? Can you take pictures of orchids, roses, dahlias and camellias that look as if they
are orchids, roses, dahlias and camellias? If you can, then all
you need to know now is what pictures to take and to whom you
will sell your photographs. You might like to learn a few tricks
of the trade at the same time.

How to Get Started

If you visit any retail nursery, you will find on the counter
colorful catalogues filled with pictures of spring or autumn
flowers, depending on the time of the year. These catalogues
are printed in bulk by one of half a dozen printers across the
country who specialize in producing this type of publication.

You probably have also received flower and shrub
catalogues through the mail. There is a difference, however,
and it is this difference that can save you time and put you on the
road to wealth.

The catalogues you receive through the mail are prepared
and mailed by a grower. He arranges to have the photographs
taken—usually by a photographer who specializes in the type of
plants grown by the grower. The grower then arranges his own
printing, publication and mailing.

The only way you will be able to get this type of work is by
making a personal presentation to the grower at the right time,
and proving that you can do better than the photographer whose
service he presently employs.

On the other side of the coin is the printer who circulates
catalogues in bulk to the retail nurseries. This printer usually

has a library of transparencies, and although many of the pictures (separations, as the printer would call them) are used year after year, this type of publisher continually adds to his library in order to keep it up-to-date.

A study of the nursery trade magazines and visits to local nurseries will provide you with the names and addresses of some of these printers. Write to these printers enclosing a few samples of your work, and state that you specialize in horticultural photography. Before this type of printer or publisher will give you work, you have to assure him that you know the difference between flowers and weeds.

Don't mention fees at this time. The printer will soon let you know what he is prepared to pay, usually between $40 and $65 a shot. At that time you may decide whether or not you wish to accept.

There are other printers who use flower pictures. Publishers of calendars will buy picture sets. You will find that they prefer to receive about two dozen transparencies from which they can select twelve. Many magazines will use color transparencies of flowers for use as cover pictures.

You stand a better chance of selling your pictures if you observe a couple of tips from professional flower photographers:

1. Use four by five inch transparencies if possible. In any case, never use a size smaller than 2 1/4 x 2 1/4 inches.
2. Place a piece of blue or gray card behind the bloom being photographed in order to avoid a confusing background of leaves and other blossoms.
3. Try to select a bloom which is in shade or arrange to do your photography on a day that is overcast. Bright sunshine does emphasize the brilliance of colors, but sometimes a transparency with excessive contrast does not reproduce as well as a transparency with greater tonal range.
4. As your work becomes known and your reputation grows, gradually start to specialize. Many financially successful

flowers— roses, orchids, chrysanthemums, dahlias, camellias and azaleas—require special techniques which can only be gained with experience.

If you can claim to be able to achieve eye-catching, compelling pictures of these commercial flowers, there will never be a shortage of work.

It may come as a surprise to you to discover that many of the close-up pictures of flowers that you see in nursery catalogues are taken in the studio. This procedure is known as table-top photography, and is a field all to itself.

THE TREMENDOUS MARKET FOR TABLE-TOP PHOTOS

Maureen G. was a research chemist in the aerospace industry. Her hobby was photography and her special interest was the taking of table-top pictures. That is to say, the photography of subjects small enough to be arranged on a table.

Later, as the government eased back on its aerospace programs, Maureen was thankful that her spare-time hobby could be quickly turned into a spare-time moneymaker. By following the steps she took, perhaps we can analyze how she set about making money from those table-top pictures.

How to Get Started

Maureen lived with her husband in a small, two-bedroom house on the outskirts of Los Angeles. At first, her pictures were simply of people and places—learning process. One day, however, her imagination was fired by a clump of wild oats growing beside her house.

After a number of attempts to get the pictures the way she visualized them, she eventually pulled the oats from the ground and took them indoors. There, on her kitchen table, and with the aid of some cellophane tape and styrofoam, she was able to arrange the slender stems exactly as she wanted them.

Although she was able to get the pictures she wanted by means of the light coming through the kitchen window, Maureen made a mental note that her next expenditure would be on two or three photo lights and stands.

Table-top photography became an absorbing interest. Maureen photographed flowers, glass statuettes, jewelry and insects. She began turning her imagination loose. She tried putting water in a baking tray and pouring oil on the surface—making a constantly changing pattern of multi-colored designs.

She began to build small sets with wood and cardboard. Plastic knights on horseback would be photographed charging down lowered drawbridges in front of formidable-looking castles. Futuristic rockets would be launched from science fiction launching pads. Palm trees and native huts dotted the sandy beaches of tropical islands set in an azure blue sea made from colored casting resin.

During one of the aerospace industry lay-offs, Maureen sent some of her table-top pictures to advertising agencies and paperback publishers. Her creative skill quickly paid dividends. Orders for specially constructed pictures poured in and today Maureen's photographs can be seen on calendars, the covers of books and as spectacular advertising photographs.

With one of her bedrooms converted to a miniature studio, Maureen puts her leisure time to very good use. Over a period of time she has gathered together a collection of some very specialized equipment. The collection includes baby spotlights, miniature floodlights, tiny tripods and a rear projection unit small enough to pack into a suitcase. There are also sheets of glass and plastic, backgrounds, shooting platforms and a large assortment of colored fabrics.

Maureen's assignments have included requests for an avalanche thundering down toward a stricken village; oranges with big smiles and laughing eyes, wearing party hats and sitting around a table with a birthday cake in the center; and a gnarled, weather-beaten hand holding a foaming tankard of beer.

Within the confines of her small studio, Maureen has photographed plane crashes, train wrecks and automobile accidents. She is currently working on an assignment from an advertising agency representing an insurance company. With the help of her husband she is constructing and photographing an impression of the San Francisco earthquake.

The type of photography in which Maureen specializes can also be used to earn money in a different way, and it is a way which you may find very intriguing.

HOW TO WIN PHOTOGRAPHIC COMPETITIONS

If there was ever a way to make money in your spare time, photographic competitions must surely be one of the best. There is undoubtedly an element of luck as there is with most competitions, but with a little planning and a knowledge of the best way to tackle photographic competitions, there is no reason why you shouldn't have expense paid trips to the Bahamas or Hawaii.

Some of the photographic competitions offer cash prizes, but most of them offer photographic equipment, expense paid vacations or prizes such as automobiles, color televisions, boats and motorcycles.

Whatever the prizes, they are invariably well worth winning. If they are not cash, they can readily be converted to cash and, if approached correctly, photographic competitions can be an enjoyable way of earning a steady spare-time income.

How to Get Started

Begin by understanding the reason for the competition. This will provide a direct answer as to the type of pictures that will win. In order to understand the reason, you must know who is sponsoring the competition. For example, if a manufacturer of photographic film is sponsoring the competition, he is probably doing so to increase sales of his product.

The manufacturer's increase in sales can come from two directions: (1) By making the photography-minded public aware of his product and (2) By preferring that the winning photos in the competition are taken with his material.

Although in most photographic competitions the sponsor's objective is an increase in sales, there are competitions with different objectives. A city council may wish to publicize a town as a holiday resort. A photographic competition may be one of the features of a state fair or pageant. There are also trade shows, particularly photographic trade shows, where visitors are encouraged to take photographs—even to the extent of the sponsors providing live models as an added attraction.

Once you know the reason for the competition, you can start planning the photographs. However, there is one important step you must take before you start planning. You must read and understand the rules of the competition.

The rules will tell you what form the finished pictures must take—black and white, color prints or transparencies—and they will tell you the size required. They will also tell you where your pictures must be sent and they will state the final date by which your pictures must be received. There may be other qualifications and, if there are, you must be aware of them.

Now, with all this information in hand, you can start planning your pictures. Put yourself in the place of the sponsors of the competition and ask yourself what type of pictures you would want. What type of subject matter would be desirable and in which way should that subject matter be presented?

For example, let us suppose that the rules state that any type of subject matter would be acceptable and the sponsors are the manufacturers of baby products. In this case, at least one of your entries must be a baby picture. If the competition is part of a state fair or pageant, it is highly probable that the winning pictures will be part of next year's publicity, so your entries must be suitable for publicity releases.

Winners in photographic competitions usually have several things in common. First, their pictures are in the style of pictures that are easily seen. That is to say, the subject matter is clear and distinct. There is no confusion of detail.

Second, they are original in concept. Perhaps it is an everyday subject photographed from an unusual angle or at an unusual time—a cat chasing a dog, a clown crying or birds migrating against a fiery sunset.

Third, the winning prints are technically perfect and free from mechanical defects.

Fourth, the winning pictures are always within the rules set up for the competition.

All in all, it is important to make a point of studying pictures which have won previous competitions. The knowledge gained in entering and winning competitions can be used to great advantage in the field of advertising photography.

HOW TO CRASH THE ADVERTISING MARKETS

The winning pictures of photographic competitions are often used for advertising purposes. The appeal that won the approval of the competition judges is the same appeal that the general public appreciates. So if you know how to take eye-catching pictures, have a sense of publicity, and think you can take pictures which will promote products and events, all that remains is to get the assignments.

Let's understand right from the beginning, that getting into the field of advertising photography isn't easy. It is highly competive and requires a fine degree of technical ability. It is, however, a market you can crack, one you can tackle in your spare time and, above all, it is fantastically profitable. If you can reach the top in advertising photography, you can name your own fee.

Worth trying for? Of course. And remember, if it was easy to become established in this field, there would be so many people taking pictures that the fees would be hardly worth troubling about.

How to Get Started

We must assume you can take pictures which catch people's attention. People flipping through the pages of a magazine must feel compelled to take a second look at your picture. We must also assume you can follow instructions given by a manufacturer on his advertising agent. For instance, if you are asked by a swimwear manufacturer to photograph an attractive woman in a bikini, the photograph must show that bikini to its greatest advantage. No matter how dramatic that pounding surf, or how breathtaking the sun dropping down like a ball of fire into a flaming sea, that manufacturer wants to see his bikini.

Having made these assumptions, there are only two hurdles to leap:

1. Getting the work.
2. Hanging on to the accounts after you've succeeded in winning them.

Let's begin with the first hurdle. Work can come to you from just two sources—the manufacturer or his agent. Under the heading of manufacturer, we must also include civic bodies, service clubs, hospitals and other similar groups that are seeking publicity. Under the heading of agents, we must include advertising agents, public relations departments, printers, and friends and relatives.

You can go after the work personally or by mail. As a spare-time project you may find it difficult to obtain sufficient time from your regular employment to be able to visit the sources of the work you seek.

If you have the time, your next step is to gather a portfolio of samples of your work, telephone for an appointment and then get out there and tell them how good you are. If a personal visit is out of the question, then sending your samples by mail is the only answer. There are many well-known photographers who live in remote areas and a lot of their work is transacted through the mails.

One of the best approaches to working through the mails is to send finished work on a speculative basis. If the photographs you take are such that they could cover a wide range of subjects, any good advertising agency can add copy which will tie the picture to the product.

For example, if you submitted a series of landscapes, fields of wheat, blue skies and puffy white clouds with a background of snow-capped mountains, you've submitted pictures which have considerable sales potential. The advertising agency can tie in such pictures to insurance companies which specialize in farming policies; to manufacturers of farming equipment, pesticides and fertilizers; and to any manufacturer who mails out advertising calendars.

In mailing out such pictures, you should offer a wide selection of subjects and enclose a stamped, self-addressed envelope for their return. The fees you charge for a one-time use of such pictures can range from a base of $50 to several hundred dollars.

How do you determine what your pictures are worth? Leave it to the advertising agent. He is very aware of current prices and, if he is a responsible businessman, he will know that by encouraging you with appropriate payment, you will continue to supply him with pictures that will please his clients.

When you have reached this position—when your reputation is strong enough to get you assignments together with top fees— the speed with which you can climb to the six figure bank account will amaze you.

HOW TO BUILD A REPUTATION FOR EYE-CATCHING PHOTOS

We've already discussed the advantages of building a top-notch reputation. If you can found that reputation on your ability to produce eye-catching pictures, those steps to a spare-time million will prove to be very pleasurable steps.

Eye-catching pictures are pictures which compel you to take a second look. The driver who makes a mental note of a billboard, the reader who pauses to read an advertisement in a magazine and the person who buys a product in the supermarket because that product is attractively packaged, are but a few of those in the general public whose visual senses are attacked many times a day by eye-catching pictures. If your imagination will allow you to take pictures which stop people dead in their tracks, you may become wealthy beyond measure.

How to Get Started

It is absolutely impossible to tell anyone how to take eye-catching pictures. For that matter, it is impossible to describe an eye-catching picture or explain why it is compelling. There are rules of composition, but it seems that people with the ability to make pictures shout a message yet follow no rules.

Therefore, we must tackle the problem from another angle. To do so, let us divide the problem into three parts:

1. Assessing the requirements.
2. Taking the photograph.
3. Selling the photograph.

1. While it may be almost impossible to explain how to take eye-catching pictures, we can at least make sure that your efforts are turned in the right direction.

Before you can even begin visualizing the projected photograph, you must know: Who is going to use the picture, why they are going to use it, how they are going to use it and where it will be used. Sometimes you also have to know when it will be used.

When you have accumulated and assessed this information, you can go ahead and turn loose your imagination. Scheme, plan, dream and arrange the picture to provide you with a finished product which will compel people to look at it.

2. If you know how the photograph is going to be used, you will know whether you are going to take black and white pictures, color prints or color transparencies.

The work must be technically perfect. If your picture is out of focus or blurred, it must be because you intended it that way. You must be master of your medium.

3. Selling your photographs has been covered previously, but there are a few more points worth knowing.

If your pictures are truly eye-catching, make sure that they catch the eye of the president of the company at which you are aiming. Send them directly to him.

Remember, and never forget, that a good big picture will always outsell a good small picture—size impresses. It doesn't matter how hardened the advertising executive or the art director of a large company, he or she will always be more interested when your pictures are of a size which hits them in the eye.

Taking eye-catching pictures is something like trying to grab a handful of mercury—tricky, but once you learn the knack, it's easy.

Finally, when you send your pictures, or even when you show them personally, make sure that they are well-presented. If a black and white print would look outstanding mounted on a gray, coarse-grained mounting board, then for heaven's sake mount it! Never let anyone see your pictures unless they are presented in a way which will do them justice.

Sometimes a four by five inch transparency will look more impressive mounted between two cut-out black cards. Sometimes a color print will look better mounted on a card and faced with a sheet of acetate film. Again, use your imagination, but be sure that you let people know that you consider your pictures to be works of art. If you don't think your photographs are worth a flourish of presentation, no one else will think so either.

Chapter 12

How to Start a Breakaway Business

By now you will have discovered that it is possible to switch on your moneymaking skills at will. You will have learned how to examine hobbies and pastimes and find their hidden fortunes. You will know how to use mail order and direct mail to lift your bank balance into the six figure bracket, and you can now literally pull ideas out of the air at any time of the day or night—ideas worth a fortune.

Here, at the tail end of the book, is a booster—a final push to get you rolling into the land of the wealthy. Any one of these ideas can be twisted in a dozen ways to provide you with a really big spare-time income.

Garage Clearing. Ideal evening and weekend work. All you need is a truck and a classified ad. You stand to win two ways. You charge the people $10 to $50 for taking away their "junk" and, after disposing of that which is truly junk, the remainder can be sold at swap meets or through a small "odds and ends" store.

Carpet and Rug Cleaning. All that is necessary is the equipment and the time. To get started, rent the equipment. Base your charges on a rate of $10 per hour.

Hydroponics. The science of growing plants without soil and using chemical plant food. Read about it in the library. There are countless opportunities in this field ranging from compounding the plant food to selling the produce and from automatic feeding systems to building special greenhouses.

Detergent Manufacturing. The basic chemicals are readily obtainable from chemical supply houses. From these chemicals you can manufacture a multitude of products ranging from rug cleaners to pet shampoos and from automobile cleaners to industrial strength factory floor washes.

Pest Control. Read up on this one. To some it may seem an unpleasant project, but it is actually an enormous profit builder.

Refrigeration Repair. There is a tremendous amount of work in this field. You will need an investment in equipment and some training through a correspondence course or a local trade college. Refrigeration maintenance is one of the most solid steps to a spare-time fortune.

Costume Making. An opportunity to specialize. Direct your talents at local theater groups and grow with your reputation.

Locksmith and Keycutting. For this you will need basic equipment and some training, but there is a steady demand for the services of a competent locksmith. The instruction can come through library books or a mail order course and key cutting equipment is constantly advertised in do-it-yourself magazines and trade directories.

Door and Windowscreen Repairs. Most hardware stores do a supplementary but steady business in screen repair. Door-to-door canvassing, handbills and local newpaper advertising can bring you the business. You will need the screen material, a length of rubber trim and a small handtool that costs a dollar or two. How-to-do-it instructions come with the tool.

Glass Cutting. A similar type of business to the previous one. You could combine the two quite easily.

Garden Fountains. For this you need a few sacks of ready-mixed concrete, a few small self-priming water pumps and an imagination which will let you design and build the most attractive garden fountains anyone has ever seen. Well, maybe they don't have to be quite that exciting—but why not? You can sell them by local advertising and through garden supply stores.

Sprinkler Installation. Ideal evening and weekend work. You can rent or buy mechanized tools to make the digging easier. However, if you are starting from absolute zero, a small payment in advance from your first customer will buy you a pick and shovel as well as the pipe and fittings. The advance payment won't supply you with the muscle power—that's something you have to provide.

Garden Furniture and Ornaments. Redwood patio armchairs, lounge seats, tables and benches are not difficult to design and manufacture. Earlier in the book we discussed how to manufacture cement planters—the same techniques can be applied to many different kinds of garden ornaments.

Lampshade Making. Most of the larger cities have a wholesale supplier of lampshade fittings and materials. Wire frames, colored plastic and fireproof material are quite inexpensive, but custom-made lampshades bring an extremely good price. You will find how-to-do-it books in your library and, in many instances, books and instructions are available through stores which specialize in arts and crafts.

Puppetry. A spare-time occupation that can be divided in two—the making of puppets and the working with them.

Making puppets for sale or for use by a puppet player is a very satisfying way of earning a spare-time income, especially for someone with an active imagination and a certain amount of creative ability.

Puppet players are always in demand and if you don't think there is much money to be made in puppetry, try watching television for a little while.

Perfume Manufacture. If you have a sensitive sense of smell, the manufacture or compounding of perfumes is a most intriguing occupation. Essential oils may be obtained from importers and manufacturers, and you can obtain their names and addresses through your public library.

The outlets for your products are nationwide and the demand is continuous. Although you could not compete on the same advertising level as the "big guns," word-of-mouth advertising is the most powerful of all.

It is worth remembering that a world-renowned men's hair cream was originated by two brothers working out of their garage.

Moss Growing. Here is a really obscure spare-time occupation. If you can grow a strong, hardy and rich green moss, people who make planter floral arrangements for banks, hospitals, corporation reception rooms and the like will buy as much moss as you can supply.

Store Window Artwork. Here is another ideal spare-time occupation for the person with artistic inclination. There is always plenty of work with shops holding "sales" and "specials".

During each of the holidays the demand for window decoration increases—at Easter and Christmas you could work 24 hours a day and still only scratch the surface.

Jewelry for Dolls. This has the potential of being developed into a big, specialized business. Starting it as a spare-time venture would be quite inexpensive. Copper wire, beads, rhinestones and plastic waste could be fashioned into jewelry to delight the heart of any little girl.

Letterhead Designing. This is an extremely high-paying occupation. If you have the skill and an eye for design, letterhead designing pays very big money. The biggest hurdle is getting the work. The secret is to watch the announcements section of your local newspaper and to make personal contact with people who are registering a new business name.

Research for Authors. Many professional writers hate the mechanics of their trade. Yet all facts about which they write, especially in non-fiction articles, should be verified. Sometimes writers feel that pausing to do research will break their flow of words. Sometimes deadlines create problems.

If you think that library detective work is an interesting way of spending your spare time, try placing an ad in a writers' magazine, announcing your services. Fees are by negotiation on a time and results basis.

Professional Fund Raising. Although the proceeds of some charities are donated entirely to those charities, there are others which set aside a portion of their funds for the payment of officers and for expenses involved in the collection of more funds. Professional fund raisers are a cross between public relations officers and astute business people.

Have you any ideas on how to raise funds for hospitals, sick children, pets and the aged? If you have, make an appointment and speak to the chairperson of the fund raising committee of the charity you would like to help.

Fake Antiques. There is no deceit intended. A lot of people and many businesses buy antiques which they know are not genuine. They buy them merely because these objects make excellent room decor and the buyers just can't afford the real thing.

Manufacturers of mobile homes decorate their display models. Large stores decorate their windows. Photographers and film studios build sets. All of these and many more are buyers of fake antiques.

Typewriter Repair. All you need are some tools of the trade, a course from a correspondence school or books from a library, and you're into a business which will take you directly into the big money brackets.

In nearly all spare-time projects you are faced with three distinct hurdles which you must surmount:

- •Deciding on the venture.
- •Getting the customers.
- •Carrying out the work.

In all honesty, none of these hurdles are too difficult for you to leap. And on the other side of those hurdles you will find incredible amounts of money and, perhaps even more important, the tremendous satisfaction of achievement. Start taking these three spare-time steps now. That million dollars is there, but it is waiting for you to take the first step. Take it.

Index